IMAGES OF W

THE BATTLE FOR
WARSAW 1939–1945

Members of the Polish Home Army fighting in Warsaw, 1944.

IMAGES OF WAR

THE BATTLE FOR WARSAW 1939–1945

RARE PHOTOGRAPHS FROM WARTIME ARCHIVES

ANTHONY TUCKER-JONES

Pen & Sword
MILITARY

AN IMPRINT OF PEN & SWORD BOOKS LTD.
YORKSHIRE – PHILADELPHIA

First published in Great Britain in 2020 by
Pen & Sword Military
an imprint of
Pen & Sword Books Ltd
Yorkshire – Philadelphia

Copyright © Pen & Sword Books 2020

ISBN 978 1 52674 150 9

A CIP catalogue record for this book is available from the British Library.

Typeset in 12/14.5 Gill Sans by
Aura Technology and Software Services, India

Printed and bound by CPI Group (UK) Ltd, Croydon CR0 4YY

Pen & Sword Books Ltd incorporates the imprints of Pen & Sword Aviation, Pen & Sword Family History, Pen & Sword Maritime, Pen & Sword Military, Pen & Sword Discovery, Wharncliffe Local History, Wharncliffe True Crime, Wharncliffe Transport, Pen and Sword Select, Pen and Sword Military Classics, Leo Cooper, The Praetorian Press, Remember When, Seaforth Publishing and Frontline Publishing.

For a complete list of Pen & Sword titles please contact

PEN & SWORD BOOKS LIMITED
47 Church Street, Barnsley, South Yorkshire, S70 2AS, England
E-mail: enquiries@pen-and-sword.co.uk
Website: www.pen-and-sword.co.uk

Or

PEN AND SWORD BOOKS
1950 Lawrence Rd, Havertown, PA 19083, USA
E-mail: Uspen-and-sword@casematepublishers.com
Website: www.penandswordbooks.com

Contents

Introduction

During the Second World War the city of Warsaw had misery after misery heaped upon it. The Nazi invasion sparked conflict across Europe and the fate of Poland became a matter of warped ideological principle. Despite their promises, in reality the Western Allies were never in a position to safeguard Warsaw or indeed influence its future. The latter controversially fell to the Soviet Union. Tragically Warsaw became the scene of regular fighting throughout the conflict. Once known as the 'Paris of the North', it became a devastated ruin.

This book is designed to provide a visual introduction to the five brutal battles that were fought in and around Warsaw. Each proved to be dramatic, decisive and bloody. The first occurred in 1939 with the defeat of the Polish army; the second was sparked by the Jewish ghetto uprising in 1943; the third saw the Red Army beaten back at the very gates of the city in the summer of 1944; the fourth was fought at the same time when the Polish Home Army unsuccessfully tried to liberate Warsaw from the Nazis; and the fifth saw the Soviets finally oust the weakened German garrison in early 1945.

The first battle for the Polish capital in the summer of 1939 culminated in Poland's surrender to Nazi Germany and led to five long years of occupation. The country as a political entity was expunged from the face of the earth. The Polish government fled into exile in London. It was aghast that the Soviet Union had occupied eastern Poland at the same time and then massacred Polish army officers. Its relations with Stalin remained strained throughout the war.

Stalin had a long memory and a score to settle with the Poles; in 1920 they had defeated the Red Army. He wanted to destroy the basis for any future opposition to the Soviet occupation of eastern Poland, which would act as a buffer against Germany. Stalin had acted swiftly. When Poland was cynically partitioned under the terms of the Nazi-Soviet Non-Aggression Pact, 130,000 Polish officers and men immediately fell into the hands of the Red Army. In total some 250,000 Polish soldiers were eventually moved into the Soviet Union as prisoners of war.

Stalin rounded up every Polish officer in his part of pre-war Poland (now western Ukraine and western Byelorussia) and in early 1940 his henchman, Beira, ruthlessly organised their slaughter. In April–May 1940 15,000 Polish officers and policemen were evacuated from camps at Kozielski, Starobielsk and Ostachkov and turned over to the NKVD in the Smolensk, Kharkov and Kalinin regions.

After Hitler invaded the Soviet Union in June 1941 the Polish government in exile signed an agreement with Moscow. Its provisions included raising a Polish army in the Soviet Union. However, of the 15,000 Polish officers held by the Soviets only 350–400 reported for duty. Like the Kulaks and Red Army officers before them, the Polish officer class had been ruthlessly liquidated.

Stalin's duplicity in his treatment of Poland and the Polish army knew no bounds. In December 1941 Generals Wladyslaw Sikorski and Wladyslaw Anders and the Polish ambassador met with Stalin to discuss the issue of the whereabouts of approximately 4,000 named Polish officers who had been deported to Soviet prisons and labour camps. Stalin initially claimed rather disingenuously that they had escaped to Manchuria. He then changed tack, suggesting they had been released, adding: 'I want you to know that the Soviet Government has not the slightest reason to retain even one Pole.' What he meant was even one living Pole.

Hitler announced he had found the mass grave of 3,000–4,000 Polish officers in the forest of Katyn near Smolensk in April 1943. The Germans continued to dig, unearthing an estimated 10,000 bodies and Hitler set up a Committee of Inquiry, which 'proved' the Poles had been shot in 1940 by the NKVD. The Soviets dismissed the claim as propaganda, calling it 'revolting and slanderous fabrications'.

The German discovery strained even further Soviet-Polish relations. This enabled Stalin to undermine the validity of the Polish government in exile in London as a prelude to establishing a communist government in Warsaw. On retaking Smolensk, the Soviets set up their own commission, which stated categorically that the Polish officers had been killed in 1941 while road building for the Germans. As far as Stalin was concern Poland came within his sphere of influence and he had every intention of it remaining so.

After the Nazi occupation of Poland its factories and railways served the German war effort on the Eastern Front. Crucially Polish partisan attacks on the railways delayed the delivery of vital German winter clothing during the desperate winter of 1941/42, much to the fury of General Heinz Guderian who watched his men freeze to death on the road to Moscow. This was followed by the horrific Jewish ghetto uprising in the spring of 1943. It was systematically and brutally supressed by Heinrich Himmler's SS troops. This proved to be a taste of things to come.

The Polish Home Army valiantly attempted to secure Warsaw in the summer of 1944. This was initially quite successful but Hitler and Himmler refused to relinquish the city, despite the proximity of the Red Army. They defeated the Red Army's efforts to cut through to the city resulting in a massive tank battle with the Waffen-SS. This left the Polish Home Army on its own for two whole months. After cutting it off from outside help, the SS brutally crushed the Poles. The survivors were forced to surrender and the city was needlessly flattened in a wanton act of revenge.

The failure of the Warsaw Rising condemned the Polish Home Army to destruction and consigned the country to communist rule. After being the scene of four battles, Warsaw was finally liberated by the Red Army and Polish communist forces in mid-January 1945. They proceeded to install a communist government in defiance of the Polish government in exile in Britain. Poland exchanged one form of occupation for another and became part of the Soviet bloc.

Photograph Sources

These public domain images have been sourced from the Fortepan photo archive, the Polish National Digital Archive, US archives, including the National Archives and Records Administration, and the author's collection. Many of the Jewish ghetto images are courtesy of the infamous *The Stroop Report* (*The Jewish Quarter of Warsaw is no More!*). This contains fifty-three photographs taken by a number of individuals including members of the German Propaganda Kompanie nr 689. When Stroop was captured by the Americans at the end of the war, he was found to be in possession of a further forty-five photographs. Combined these present a gruesome record of the atrocities committed in the Warsaw Ghetto.

Chapter One

Warsaw '39

In the face of Nazi aggression, Marshal Edward Rydz-Śmigly and the commanders of the Polish Army faced a terrible dilemma in 1939. The Polish General Staff, in the War Ministry Building in Saxon Square, Warsaw, saw Russia as Poland's historic enemy not Germany. They had always hoped that Germany might be an ally. The assumption was that Poland would fight a coalition war against the Soviet Union. Certainly Stalin had made no secret of the fact that he wished to restore the old Tsarist frontiers.

Ironically General Romer, the Polish Chief of Staff, looking East had said, 'Our principles must be taken from the lesson of the Napoleonic Wars, from the first battles of the World War (particularly on the Eastern Front), and from the last Russo-Polish War. Our salvation lies in a war of movement.' The problem was that the Polish Army was not mobile. Furthermore, during the 1930s Polish dictator Marshal Józef Pilsudski had resisted German pressure to support a campaign against the Soviet Union.

Warsaw, on the Vistula River, represented the strategic heart of Poland, but the Polish military could not concentrate their resources in defence of the capital. Holding the Vistula would have provided a natural defensive barrier against the German armed forces. If they did, though, it meant abandoning Poland's western frontier and the port of Danzig on the Baltic Sea, which sat at the head of the Polish Corridor. This was sandwiched between Germany and East Prussia – the latter also being German territory. Danzig was designated an independent 'free city' and almost entirely populated by Germans whom Hitler wanted back in the fold of the Fatherland. Furthermore, the Polish army's vital railheads, the industrial centres and the vast Silesian coalfields were all west of the Vistula. This forced the small regular Polish army to deploy near the German frontier.

On paper at least Rydz-Śmigly's forces appeared formidable consisting of about 30 first-line divisions, 10 reserve divisions and 11 cavalry brigades. The Polish army had 1.75 million men, but this included large numbers of reservists who had not been fully mobilised. They were supported by 500 mainly obsolete tanks and 745 aircraft. The latter were controlled by the Polish army and navy, as there was no separate air force. Almost half of Polish aircraft were with training schools and the reserves. Operational units only included 159 fighters, 118 light bombers and 36 heavier bombers. Much of their equipment dated from the First World War. These numbers meant nothing because the Poles were not given time to deploy their aircraft.

The tiny Polish navy, controlled from its headquarters in Warsaw, was in no position to help the capital. It consisted of just four flotillas, two of which were river based and a small naval air force. Its key vessels were four destroyers and five submarines as well as half a dozen minesweepers and a number of other support vessels. These were no match for the combined might of the German Luftwaffe and Kriegsmarine. Once tensions were escalating with Germany the Polish navy decided under the Peking Plan to send its three most modern destroyers to Britain.

Britain and France, anxious that Poland should not provoke Hitler, had called on the Poles to delay their mobilisation. As a result thousands of reservists were on the way to their units when Hitler attacked. To complicate matters for the Polish army, some 30 per cent of those living in Poland were not ethnic Poles. There were at least half a dozen large minorities including 2 million Germans. Others included 1 million Belorussians and almost 4 million Ukrainians. In the event Poland mobilised thirty-five divisions, but few of these were full strength.

The Poles' defensive plans were delusional. Lacking mobility, they chose to fight near the frontier. This left them exposed, especially in the Polish Corridor. It also meant that they had to defend a 1,750-mile-long border. The Poles had also created a special assault group with which to attack East Prussia, where German troops were massing.

Adolf Hitler's Blitzkrieg, or Lightning War, rolled into Poland at 0445 hours on 1 September 1939. Beforehand the Luftwaffe smashed the Polish air capability and destroyed Poland's railways. The latter greatly hampered the mobilisation of the Polish army. Hitler's plan was to take Warsaw and defeat the Poles ready for an invasion of the Soviet Union. To stop Stalin intervening Hitler had agreed that the Red Army could occupy eastern Poland. Hitler struck Poland with 44 divisions, which included 6 panzer and 4 light divisions with 1,700 tanks supported by 2,000 aircraft. Despite dense fog at 0600 hours, the Luftwaffe bombed Warsaw without warning.

The Luftwaffe did not catch all of the Polish aircraft on the ground. At the end of August, the Poles had prudently redeployed their planes to emergency air strips. What the Germans caught were not airworthy or obsolete airframes. The Poles saved their fighters, 86 bombers and 150 reconnaissance aircraft, to resist the Luftwaffe in the coming week. The Polish designs and numbers were, though, inferior to the Germans and could not prevent the Luftwaffe gaining air supremacy.

On the German side Colonel General von Bock's Army Group North consisted of the Third and Fourth armies. The latter was deployed opposite Danzig and the Polish Corridor. General von Bock's 3rd and 19th corps were tasked with overrunning and cutting off the Corridor. The Third Army was deployed in East Prussia. It was to attack southwards towards Warsaw and southeast towards Brest-Litovsk. In total, Bock had some 630,000 men under his command.

Colonel General von Rundstedt's Army Group South, deployed in Silesia and Slovakia, comprised the Eighth, Tenth and Fourteenth armies. Rundstedt was instructed to drive towards Warsaw and form the right-hand arm of a huge pincer that was to trap Polish forces in Poznia and west of the Vistula River. While the Eight and Tenth armies headed for Lodz and the River Bzura, further south the Fourteenth Army would cross the Carpathian Mountains and drive toward Lublin. Rundstedt's forces amounted to 886,000 men.

Despite the involvement of Hiter's new panzer forces, the quality of his tanks was poor. Most of his armour consisted of the Panzer II armed with a 20mm cannon. There were few Panzer IIIs armed with an inadequate 37mm gun or Panzer IV's armed with a low-velocity 75mm support gun. However, the father of Hitler's panzerwaffe, General Heinz Guderian, was in charge of the armoured formations supporting von Bock. Through the 1930s Guderian had conducted experiments with the panzers and overseen operations in Austria and Czechoslovakia. All of which had convinced him of the power of the tank if correctly supported by aircraft, artillery and infantry. Guderian argued that the armour should be kept together so that its mobility could be capitalised on. He grouped his tanks into an armoured fist with Army Group North. However, von Rundstedt was not receptive to such progressive thinking and he split his tanks up.

To date Hitler's expansion of Germany with the reoccupation of the Rhineland, union with Austria and the seizure of Slovakia had all been accomplished without bloodshed. The conquest of Poland could only be achieved by force of arms. Hitler confirmed that. 'Further successes are impossible without shedding blood.' To defeat Warsaw, Hitler unleashed his new form of war known as Blitzkrieg. Although the German armed forces were far from ready for war, Hitler was prepared to gamble he would win. Hitler knew he had to attack before late September and October when the rains turned much of Poland into a sticky bog. Likewise, the weather would mean Poland's major rivers would be in full flood.

In the days preceding Hitler's onslaught, the Germans had deliberately made the war look like it was the Poles' fault. On 31 August 1939 Reichsführer-SS Heinrich Himmler conducted Operation Canned Goods. Twelve German convicts were dressed in Polish uniforms and then given lethal injections. Their corpses were dumped in the woods near Hochlinde, some 10 miles west of the border. A second deception operation was conducted at Geliwitz where an SS unit took over the local radio station and began broadcasting in Polish. The SS then shot a thirteenth prisoner claiming it was he who had made the broadcast. The following day Hitler announced that Polish aggression would not go unpunished.

A few days before the Nazi invasion the old German battleship *Schleswig-Holstein*, now officially a training ship, sailed into Danzig. On the morning of 1 September her 11in guns opened fire on the Polish barracks at Westerplatte overlooking the harbour. The garrison was to hold out for a week. The Luftwaffe also set about the Polish armed forces. German Heinkel III bombers flying from East Prussia attacked the Warsaw-Okecie airfield as a prelude to Operation Seaside on 1 September. This was a wholesale assault on the Polish capital. The fog meant they struggled to hit the hangars. Due to the weather, the bombers did not return until later in the day hitting Warsaw-Okecie again as well as airfields at Goclaw and Mokotow. Dive-bombers also hit Polish radio stations at Babice and Lacy.

Some thirty Polish fighters rose to meet the Germans' Me 110 escort fighters. The Poles lost five aircraft and withdrew. Although these early raids on Polish air fields were not very effective, they did severely disrupt Polish military communications. Telephone and teleprinter systems were wrecked. One of the most terrifying weapons that the Germans unleashed was the Junkers 87 dive-bomber – better known as the Stuka. Its wailing sirens fitted to its undercarriage added to the sense of panic and terror.

A second air battle took place over Warsaw on 3 September. Again, the Poles lost five fighters claiming just one German kill. However, by 1800 hours the thick fog had returned. Polish pilots also resisted over Lodz. There they lost eleven fighters and a bomber in the air and three fighters on the ground on 4 September. The Polish bomber brigade under Colonel W. Heller conducted sorties from 2 September and continued to attack German ground forces up until mid-month. By which time just a few Polish bombers were still airworthy. Some 333 Polish aircraft were lost on operations, including 82 from the bomber brigade. The Poles soon began to run out of spare parts and on 17 September the remaining serviceable aircraft were flown to Romania.

Within days of Hitler's invasion Polish defences had been penetrated. The frightened Polish population fled their homes and choked the roads with refugees. Although Britain and France declared war on Germany on 3 September, there was nothing they could really do to help. At this stage a diversionary attack on Germany's Western Frontier was simply out of the question. However, Hitler knew that speed was of the essence as he could not afford to fight a two-front war. Just after the attack on Poland he had forty-three divisions facing the French. When they declared war France only had seven divisions available for the Western Front. French troops also had to guard the borders with Italy and Spain, while another fourteen divisions were in French North Africa.

At first Poland's political and military leaders were uncertain as to the scope of Hitler's attack. Mistakenly they thought that he was simply seeking to take Danzig and liquidate the Polish Corridor. If Hitler achieved this, then perhaps the fighting would stop and the Poles would have the option of ceding territory rather than continuing the war. It soon became apparent that the whole of western Poland was under attack.

In panic the Polish government left Warsaw for Lublin on 4 September. Marshal Rydz-Śmigły and the high command followed three days later. Many Poles thought President Ignace Mosciki was a coward. He wanted Warsaw declared an open city to save it from devastation. Instead the people of Warsaw hoped if they held out long enough the British and French would force the Germans to turn West.

Poland in the late 1930s looked East rather than West when it came to its defence. The Poles' hereditary enemy since the fourteenth century was Russia rather than Germany. They had fought a long series of wars, the most recent of which was the Polish-Soviet War during 1919–21. Soviet propaganda, such as this Bolshevik poster from 1920, made the Poles look like the oppressors.

Polish defences outside Warsaw, 1920. Poland triumphed against Russia at the Battle of Warsaw and gained a slice of Ukraine. However, the Polish army remained rooted in the past and was not forward thinking.

Polish troops in Kiev during the Polish-Soviet War. Poland supported Ukraine's aspirations of independence from Moscow. By the late 1930s Poland's population included nearly 4 million Ukrainians.

During the 1920s and 1930s Poland was ruled by Marshal Józef Pilsudski, who resisted an alliance with Germany against the Soviet Union.

By the late 1930s Marshal Edward Rydz-Śmigly was the second most powerful man in Poland after the president. He was faced with a difficult strategic situation when it came to the defence of Warsaw.

Rydz-Śmigly receiving his marshal's baton, 1936. Three years later with the Nazi invasion he was appointed commander-in-chief of all Poland's armed forces.

Marshal Rydz-Śmigly reviewing tanks. This was the image Poland like to project to the world – one of military strength.

Soviet Foreign Minister Molotov signing the Nazi-Soviet Non-Aggression Pact on 23 August 1939, with Stalin smiling in the background. This sealed the fate of Poland and paved the way for its partition.

Polish infantry on the march. The Polish army, although large, was not very manoeuvrable and had delayed its mobilisation in the summer of 1939. In the event it was able to pit thirty-five understrength divisions against forty-four German divisions. The Germans also had vastly more tanks and aircraft.

Polish light bomber and reconnaissance aircraft known as the PZL.23 Karaś. About 250 of these were built during the 1930s; less than half deployed were with combat units and the rest were held in reserve or were with training schools. Poland had no separate air force and instead the army and navy operated their own aircraft.

Poland had almost 700 two-man light tanks or tankettes built during the 1930s. The main models were the TK 3 and TK S which were derived from the British Carden-Loyd Mark VI light tank. The main difference between the two Polish models was the engine. Initially both were armed with a machine gun mounted in the front right-hand side of the hull. Some TK 3, though, had the machine gun replaced by a 20mm cannon. By 1939 eighteen infantry divisions and eleven cavalry brigades had been issued with a company of TK 3s or TK Ss. Two of the motorised cavalry brigades had two companies each.

The Polish-built 7TP light tank was based on the British Vickers-Armstrong design. Initially the Poles purchased around forty Vickers-Armstrong 6-ton Mark E tanks from England between 1932 and 1934. The first version of the 7TP had twin turrets armed with machine guns. The subsequent version had a single turret armed with a 37mm gun.

A column of Polish 7TP tanks on parade in Warsaw. The second tank from the right is an imported British Vickers 6-tonner. When the Germans invaded the Polish army had 169 7TPs, 50 Vickers tanks, 67 Renault FT-17 light tanks, 53 Renault R-35 light tanks, 700 tankettes and 100 wz 34 and wz 29 armoured cars. The Poles were in the process of building the 10TP medium tank but it was not ready in time.

Although an impressive sight, by 1939 only about 170 7TPs had been built.

The Luftwaffe's Ju 87 Stuka dive-bomber brought terror and panic to Poland on 1 September 1939. It was used to attack Polish airfields, troop concentrations and exposed lines of communication such as railways, roads and bridges.

Polish PWS 10 fighter aircraft taxiing for take-off. The Luftwaffe failed to catch the bulk of Poland's aircraft on the ground because most had been redeployed before Hitler's assault. Only eighty of this aircraft type were built in the early 1930s and were only used in a reconnaissance role.

At the end of August 1939, just before Hitler's invasion, the outnumbered Polish navy instigated the Peking Plan under which three destroyers sailed for Britain. Although the navy was attacked by the Luftwaffe during the Battle of Danzig Bay, some other vessels such as the submarine ORP *Orzel* also escaped to Britain to carry on the fight. This brand-new submarine had only been commissioned into service on 2 February 1939.

Chapter Two

The Siege

By 5 September 1939 the German 3rd Corps was in Bromberg at the base of the Polish Corridor. To the south two days later von Rundstedt was in Cracow, Poland's second city, and heading for Kielce and Lodz. The German Fourth Army moved up the Vistula towards Warsaw. The 4th Panzer Division reached the outskirts of the Polish capital on the afternoon of 8 September. The Tenth Army took Kielce as the Fourteenth Army reached Sandomierz on the junction of the Vistula and Sans rivers.

That day Molotov, the Soviet Foreign Minister, congratulated Germany 'on the entry of German troops into Warsaw'. Just after midnight von Ribbentrop, the German Foreign Minister, signalled to the German ambassador in Moscow saying the invasion of Poland was 'progressing even beyond our expectations'. He went on to ask the ambassador to find out when the Soviet Union planned to act against Poland. The following day Molotov replied, 'within the next few days'.

Behind Hitler's armies came his SS-Einsatzgruppen, or Special Task Forces. Their mission was to murder Poland's intelligentsia and its Jewish population. Admiral Wilhelm Canaris, head of Hitler's military intelligence service, was reporting by the end of the first week of the invasion that the SS were shooting 200 people a day. This was part of a monstrous plan to create a leaderless work force that could be exploited by Germany.

In London there was an air of unfounded optimism. General Ironside, the Chief of the Imperial General Staff, reported to the British Cabinet: 'The Poles are putting up a good fight and are defending Warsaw vigorously. Their main army is still intact. Eight divisions have been caught in the Posen salient, but it is hoped that some might break through. A line of defence has been taken up on the Vistula.'

In the Polish capital with the government gone the opposition parties formed the Defence of Warsaw Committee. This was headed by Stefan Starzynski, the city mayor. General Michal Tokarzewski acted as the military representative and its other members included M. Niedzialkowski of the Socialist Party and Mathew Rataj of the Peasant Party. They rallied the reservists to the defence of Warsaw. The garrison was commanded by General Walerian Czuma. A force dubbed the Warsaw Army was also put together under General Juliusz Rómmel. On 11 September Marshal Rydz-Śmigly ordered the city and Modlin fortress be held in anticipation of a counterattack by Britain and France.

Originally the German Tenth Army was supposed to push east, but it was soon apparent that the bulk of the Polish forces were still west of Warsaw. Instead the Tenth Army under Major General Walter von Reichenau was ordered to cut the Poles off from the capital. The Third Army striking from East Prussia formed the other pincer west of Warsaw. By 14 September German armour and infantry had surrounded the city.

The Luftwaffe attacked Warsaw on 13 September with over 180 aircraft. Another large-scale attack was conducted four days later. Hermann Göring, Commander-in-Chief of the Luftwaffe, ordered, 'Priority of attack shall be given to public utilities (water, gas and power sources), barracks and ammunition dumps, the *Woywod* building, citadel, ministry of war, inspectorate general, traffic centres, and known battery positions.' It seemed that nothing was to be spared.

The Polish army under General Kutrzeba in the Poznan area desperately attempted to conduct a fighting withdrawal between the Bzura and the Vistula. They were joined by other units from the Polish Corridor. Despite the Luftwaffe's efforts and the chaos on the roads, these forces managed to swing southwards across the Bzura and attack the German Eighth Army's southern advance. The German 30th Infantry Division found itself under attack by four Polish infantry divisions and two cavalry brigades and had to be rescued. In response the Germans wheeled the panzer corps that was attacking Warsaw to strike the Poles from the east. The attacks on Warsaw were put on hold. What followed became known as the Battle of the Bzura or the Battle of Kutno.

The Luftwaffe set about the Polish columns south of the Bzura near Bielawy and Piatek. It broke up the Polish advance and averted the crisis faced by the Eighth Army. The remnants of nineteen Polish divisions and three cavalry brigades were trapped in the Kutno area to the west of Warsaw and Modlin. There they were subjected to continuous air assault.

Genera Kutrzeba recalled coming 'under pulverising bombardment from the air. It was just hell on earth. The bridges were destroyed, the fords blocked, the waiting columns of men decimated.' Along with his chief of staff and another officer, they remained trapped in the village of Myszory until a lull in the bombing. After a 9-day battle, despite desperate efforts to break out, on 19 September 1939 around 170,000 Polish troops surrendered. They had suffered 20,000 dead and 32,000 wounded. Only a few survivors escaped eastwards through the Kampinoska forest to reach Modlin.

Five days earlier Guderian had reached Brest-Litovsk and subsequently linked up with Army Group South at Wlodawa. This effectively trapped all Polish forces in western Poland. East of Brzesc at Zabinka one of the Poles' few tank units was being unloaded from a train when the Germans arrived. It now only remained to destroy the last Polish pockets of resistance and take Warsaw.

On 17 September Stalin stabbed the Poles in the back and the Red Army invaded eastern Poland. One army group advanced to the north and another to the south of the impassable Pripet Marshes. Those Polish units encountered were swiftly taken prisoner. The Soviets rounded up over 200,000 Poles. Stalin was determined that the Polish army would not rise from the ashes. Around 15–20,000 Polish officers were taken to Katyn forest to the west of Smolensk and massacred. The country was divided along the Bug, San and Narew rivers.

Yet still heroic Warsaw did not give up. The German army became embroiled in tough street warfare. The civilian population dug trenches and created barricades using cars and trams. Mechanised warfare was not easily carried out in the city and the panzers were destroyed at close quarters. In response the Luftwaffe pounded the city into rubble. On 25 September 240 dive-bombers commenced attacking Warsaw from 0800 hours onwards. They were supported by thirty Ju 52 transport aircraft which were used to deliver incendiary bombs. The crews simply tossed them from the open door. During that day the Luftwaffe was able to commit over 400 bombers, dive-bombers and ground-attack aircraft to the raids. They dropped 500 tons of high explosives and 72 tons of incendiaries. The death and destruction was terrible.

In the space of just a few days the Luftwaffe destroyed huge areas of the city including the flour mills, gasworks, power stations and the reservoir. The residential areas were also showered with incendiary bombs. 'There were fires every day,' said one resident, 'we slept fully dressed with our suitcases containing the most indispensable objects next to our beds.' Although thousands of Poles volunteered, the military commission would only take those with training, which essentially meant those from the reserves and para-military organisations.

When the Germans pushed into the western suburbs they were met by petrol bombs. A member of one of the volunteer battalions recalled, 'Fighting started every evening about 6pm with our attack, and lasted till dawn.' During the day the Luftwaffe bombed their trenches and destroyed their munitions. The Poles, though, could do little to fend off the bombers and German artillery fire.

Still Britain and France did not act to save Warsaw. By 20 September France had mobilised fifty-seven divisions but this included forces defending the Maginot Line. British troops were not deployed until early October. The French dropped leaflets over Germany and conducted a few patrols. The Royal Air Force restricted its activities to attacking the German navy. Warsaw's fate was sealed. It was not until three weeks after the Polish surrender that Britain had 4 divisions comprising 158,000 men in France.

In the city ammunition, food and medical supplies ran out and on 27 September Czuma and Rómmel were forced to surrender. Some 12,000 civilians were killed during the siege. The fortress of Modlin held out another day. Just before the surrender Rómmel summoned Tokarzewski to the War Department in Pilsudski Square. He instructed Tokarzewski to set up an underground organisation to continue the struggle. By the time of Warsaw's surrender Reinhard Heydrich of the SS was claiming just 3 per cent of the Polish upper classes had escaped the Einsatzgruppen.

When the Germans occupied Warsaw they warned that anyone caught carrying a weapon of any sort or hiding weapons at home would face execution. Triumphant German units held a victory parade through Pilsudski Square. At Kock to the southeast of Warsaw 17,000 troops held out until 6 October 1939. Only 100,000 Polish soldiers, including Marshal Rydz-Śmigly, escaped to Romania along with 116 aircraft. Hitler's dramatic conquest of Poland cost him around 40,000 casualties, including 8,000 killed. He also lost 217 tanks and 285 aircraft. To Hitler this was a small price to pay for bringing Poland to its knees.

The stretched Polish armed forces were overwhelmed. When Hitler invaded Poland his tank force included 1,445 Panzer I light tanks.

German armour used this very distinctive white cross as a recognition symbol during the invasion of Poland. It was designed to avoid friendly fire.

The Panzer I command tank variant in Poland. The Panzers vastly outnumbered Poland's tank force.

Opposite above: The Polish 7TP light tank was better armed than Hitler's Panzer I and II. However, Poland's tank forces were no match for Hitler's rapidly moving Blitzkrieg.

Opposite middle: Polish 75mm guns preparing for action. The speed of Hitler's Blitzkrieg ensured that the Polish army was swiftly surrounded in a matter of weeks.

Opposite below: A Polish horse-drawn 120mm howitzer. Such units were easy prey for the Luftwaffe, especially the Ju 87 Stuka dive-bomber.

A Polish infantryman studies a propaganda poster on the streets of Warsaw. The poster optimistically reads 'To Arms – United, we will defeat the enemy'. Despite the presence of the soldier, these women and children faced a miserable future. On 11 September 1939 Marshal Rydz-Śmigly ordered the city to be held, and three days later it was completely surrounded by the Germans.

Above: A despondent Polish boy among the desolation of Warsaw. The city was first bombed on 1 September 1939, although poor weather hampered the Luftwaffe. It was then attacked on an almost daily basis until the garrison surrendered on 27 September. Particularly heavy raids took place on 13, 17 and 25 September. The latter involved over 400 aircraft.

Opposite above: Warsaw's Royal Castle ablaze after German shelling on 17 September 1939. The German rules of engagement seemed to have no limits.

Opposite below: This Polish soldier is firmly dug in. Warsaw's garrison was commanded by General Walerian Czuma, while the outer defences came under the control of General Juliusz Rómmel.

An abandoned Polish wz 34 armoured car. Only eighty-six of these were built in 1934. Its armament consisted of either one short 37mm gun or one 7.92mm machine gun in the turret. Along with a few of the older wz 29, it was deployed by the reconnaissance squadrons with the cavalry brigades. The wz 34 only had 6mm of armour so did not last very long in combat.

A Polish 105mm gun. Once the bulk of the trapped Polish army had surrendered west of Warsaw the city was on its own.

General Heinz Guderian with Brigadier Semyon Krivoshein of the Red Army in Brest-Litovsk. Stalin invaded eastern Poland on 17 September 1939, taking over 200,000 prisoners. Poland lay prostrate.

Desperate times. When Warsaw's garrison surrendered on 27 September 1939, food shortages were such that the civilian population resorted to eating horse meat.

Hitler's forces did not have it all their way. This Panzer I was destroyed during the Polish campaign. In total Hitler lost 8,000 killed, 217 tanks and 285 aircraft.

A German Panzer II sporting the Polish campaign symbol. The Luftwaffe and panzers reigned supreme in Poland and crushed the Polish army in a matter of weeks.

On 4 October 1939 Hitler ordered Warsaw's Royal Castle be blown up. The building was gutted and reduced to a shell, its treasures desecrated. The city was to be blighted by widespread cultural vandalism.

The National Museum in Warsaw was damaged during the siege and after the Polish surrender its treasures were also looted by the Germans. The city's university was turned into a German barracks.

Chapter Three

Guderian's Trains

From the start Hitler and his generals knew they had to capture Warsaw quickly. A pre-war study had shown that Germany's oil stocks and synthetic oil production would only enable them to fight for seven months. The bulk of its key raw materials were imported including 99 per cent of its bauxite, 80 per cent of its rubber, 75 per cent of its oil and 70 per cent of its tin. Notably Germany was reliant on imports from the Soviet Union, Hungary and Romania. Under the provisions of the Nazi-Soviet Non-Aggression Pact, Stalin had ended up with possession of all the oilfields in southeastern Poland, although he had undertaken to supply Germany with 30,000 tons of oil a year. Originally the Baltic coast had been allocated to Germany, but Stalin was determined to reassert Russia's historic control over Lithuania.

Following the surrender of Warsaw, the country was swiftly erased from the map. Hitler occupied western and central Poland up to the River Bug, the rest was left to Stalin. Silesia along with the northwestern half of Poland became part of Germany. The population was deported and the houses, farms and factories were given to Germans.

What was left became a German vassal state called the General-Government and Cracow, not Warsaw, became its capital. Hitler and his cronies knew that Warsaw would be a focus for resistance. 'We have in this country one point from which all evil derives: namely Warsaw,' claimed Hans Frank, the German Governor General of Poland. Those with an eye for history knew there had been a Warsaw uprising against Russian rule in 1794. Another had been started by the cadets of the Warsaw School of Infantry in 1830. Warsaw was the focal point for yet another rising in 1863 and again in 1904–7.

Hitler visited Warsaw just once on 5 October 1939 to take the salute of the victorious Eighth Army. Afterwards he toured the Belvedere Palace and then rushed back to Berlin. He had little regard for the Polish people. 'The Führer's verdict of the Poles is damning,' noted Nazi Propaganda Minister Joseph Goebbels, 'Their capacity for intelligent judgement is absolutely nil . . .'. On the eve of the invasion Hitler had told his generals: 'I have sent my [SS] Death's Head units to the East with the order to kill without mercy men, women and children of the Polish race or language.

Only in such a way will we win the Lebensraum [living space] that we need. Who, after all, speaks today of the annihilation of the Armenians?'

Governor Frank was determined to crush the spirit of Warsaw, as the city was the cultural heart of Poland. Frank was of course right because Major General Tokarzewski had given an undertaking to form a secret army. He had promised to 'assume full responsibility for the organization of armed resistance against the occupying powers, and the preparation of the country's moral and physical readiness to begin open warfare when the conditions were favourable'. On 24 October 1939 Warsaw was placed under the control of Ludwig Fischer.

The Poles fared far worse than the Western Europeans under Nazi rule and their fate bore little similarity with that of Denmark or the Netherlands or even Vichy France. The Germans not only carved up Poland with the Soviet Union but also split it up further. Some parts were annexed, while others were incorporated into the Reichkommissariate of 'Ostland' and 'Ukraine', while the remains were administered as the General-Government. The Germans retained up to ½ million police and troops in Poland. The Poles resisted from the start with the Armia Krajowa, or Home Army, coming into official existence in 1942, with a maximum strength of 400,000 men.

Many of the people from the Polish lands taken by Germany were shipped to the General-Government by the SS. Anyone who resisted or tried to runaway was shot. Cities such as Poznan were emptied. First the inhabitants were told to clean their homes and leave supplies for the incoming Germans. The Germans embarked on a needless campaign of cultural vandalism, closing universities and looting and ransacking art galleries, libraries and museums.

Even before the invasion German industrial experts had earmarked those Polish factories that would be vital for Hitler's war effort. In particular Warsaw was a potential powerhouse. There was a massive workforce there comprising 90,000 factory employees as well as 23,000 independent artisan workshops. They had to be made pliant by removing any potential resistance leaders.

The German Secret State Police, the Geheime Staatpolizei, or Gestapo for short, created lists and began to arrest people. Among the first was Mayor Stefan Starzynski and former Speaker of the Polish Parliament and leader of the Peasant Party Mathew Rataj. The Gestapo set up their headquarters in the Polish Ministry of Religion and Education in Szuch Avenue, which was renamed Strasse der Polizei. The Germans also requisitioned two Warsaw prisons to hold their political prisoners.

German managers were brought in to run Poland's factories. Among them was Walter Toebbens, who drew his workforce from the Warsaw ghetto. He shared his profits with SS Major General Odilo Globocnik, the police chief in Lublin and head of the death-camp organisation. German managers also aided the Gestapo in weeding out the less-productive workers, who were then sent to the gas chambers.

The Germans took over the state-run engineering enterprise Panstwowy Zaklad in Warsaw, which was licensed to build Polski Fiat motor vehicles. In preparation for the impending Operation Barbarossa, the invasion of the Soviet Union, 15,000 Polish pattern Panjewagen horse-drawn carts were acquired for the German infantry divisions, in order to increase their mobility. The Germans also made use of Polish small arms such as the 9mm Radom wz 35 pistol, which entered Wehrmacht service as the P 35(p).

The deliberate obstruction of Warsaw's rail network by Polish resistance first began to make itself felt during the winter of 1941. The results had a major impact with German troops slowly freezing to death outside Moscow. When General Guderian visited the 112th and 167th Infantry divisions in Russia on 14 November 1941 he was appalled to discover a complete lack of winter clothing. Many men were suffering frostbite and their vehicles were immobilised. Guderian was furious, as he had requested appropriate clothing in September and October, and he took steps to find out what was going on.

The Army Quartermaster General insisted winter clothing had been issued. After making some telephone calls Guderian discovered it had been stranded for weeks at Warsaw railway station due to a lack of trains and disruption of the lines. When Guderian saw Hitler in late December 1941 a heated argument took place over the issue. Guderian pointed out that the cold was causing twice as many casualties as the Red Army. Hitler accused him of not seeing the bigger picture and that winter clothing had been issued. When the Quartermaster General was summoned he confessed that the kit remained in Warsaw. The damage was done, Hitler's troops froze and a week later Guderian was relieved of his command.

In the meantime, some Polish factories were put to work for the Luftwaffe, for example, a factory in the Zoliborz district of Warsaw made airscrews until the Polish Home Army burned it to the ground on 30 September 1942. The following month the Polish resistance blew up every railway line leading out of the Polish capital. This cut vital links with the Eastern Front and stopped a crucial ammunition and supply train destined for German troops at Stalingrad.

One Polish company, ominously known as the 'Firm', with offices in Warsaw and Minsk, the Byelorussian capital, was employed to supply the Wehrmacht on the Eastern Front. In reality it indulged in several sidelines which included gun-running to Soviet partisans. Supplied with official passes, the 'Firm's' trucks were able to pass through both German and partisan lines unmolested. However, the Germans saw the Poles as little better than slaves and the best workers were sent to work in German armament factories.

During a 4-day period in January 1943 the Germans sent 35,000 men and women either to the concentration camps or to Germany to work as slave labour.

Rather than maintaining a productive work force that could have supported the German war economy, the Nazis set about destroying it. The German Arbeitsamt, or Labour Office, oversaw the deportation of nearly 2 million Polish workers to Germany. There they were treated as subhuman slaves. The Germans also set up three camps 30 miles from Warsaw to hold 'young offenders'. Around 110,000 farmers, agricultural workers and their families were also driven from their lands. Even Governor Frank came to appreciate that they were 'slaughtering the cow which they wanted to milk'. This realisation was brought about by the shattering German defeat at Stalingrad.

Fresh graves in Warsaw's Three Crosses Square opposite St Alexander's Church. In 1939 fatalities had to be buried as quickly as possible to stop the spread of disease. It would not be long before the sight of dead bodies lying in the streets was commonplace.

German troops march triumphantly through Warsaw. Hitler arrived on 5 October 1939 to take the salute of the German Eighth Army. Nazi-occupied Poland was soon placed under the control of Governor-General Hans Frank with his capital in Cracow. Ludwig Fischer was appointed Governor of Warsaw.

Among the equipment captured by the Germans was the TK S tankette. Some were recycled for internal security duties.

The new border with the Soviet Union. Under the terms of the Non-Aggression Pact signed with Germany, Stalin retained control of eastern Poland.

Warsaw and the rest of Nazi-occupied Poland soon became a police state. The former Polish capital was rapidly forced to become a German-speaking city.

Opposite above: Polish hostages being taken away. Any attacks on German units resulted in immediate reprisals. Executions started in September 1939 when German troops shot fifty-one Polish prisoners.

Opposite below: The Germans took over all of Poland's factories and these were forced to work in support of the German war effort. Warsaw alone had a labour force of over 100,000.

In Warsaw the Germans immediately began segregating the Jewish and non-Jewish population. Polish Jews and Jews from across the occupied territories were herded into the Warsaw ghetto like cattle and walled in.

A footbridge leading into the Warsaw ghetto. This consisted of two areas west of the Vistula River. The Germans also built a concentration camp within the city limits.

The Jewish Council building after the 1943 rising. The ghetto was administered by the SS-appointed Jewish Council and the Ghetto police force.

The Umschlagplatz from where Jews were shipped to Treblinka concentration camp and certain death.

The brutal German response to Polish opposition. These ten hostages were executed on 15 June 1941 in Gąbin.

Polish Jews from the Siedlice ghetto
being sent to Treblinka in late
August 1942.

Jews from the Cracow ghetto being sent to Auschwitz concentration camp.

More savagery during the occupation – the public execution of fifty-four Polish men and women in the village of Rożki, 1942.

Warsaw rabbis being questioned by SS security forces. For over three-and-a-half years the Jews cooperated with Hitler's murderous plans, until finally resisting in early 1943.

In April 1943 SS-Brigadeführer Jürgen Stroop, second from the right, was placed in charge of crushing the Warsaw ghetto uprising.

Stroop reviewing his men. They consisted of two reserve SS training battalions, cavalry and panzergrenadier units as well as Lithianian and Polish militia.

Stroop and Eastern security auxiliaries in the Umschlagplatz.

German auxiliaries examining their handiwork in the Warsaw ghetto – the murder of men, women and children.

Chapter Four

Horrors of the Ghetto

Warsaw was treated as a police state and dominated by over twenty military bases and police stations. The German garrison included some 6,000 military police by 1943. German was made the official language and the Germans controlled the media. Many buildings and streets were given German names. Apartheid became a way of life with 'Germans Only' signs springing up throughout Warsaw. Any resistance was punishable by firing squad or hanging. Governor Frank authorised the Gestapo to shoot on suspicion in the autumn of 1943.

That year Warsaw was the scene of a horrific tragedy. It occurred because of the Nazis' abhorrent anti-Semitic policies. The previous year the communist underground was becoming active and the Germans escalated the arrests, especially in the former Polish capital. Mass shootings also spiralled outside Warsaw. The Germans then decided to liquidate the Warsaw Jewish ghetto. This had not existed before the war but the Germans had started segregating the population on the basis of Jewish and non-Jewish in November 1939.

All non-Jews in the designated ghetto area were expelled and the city's Jews herded in and surrounded by a wall. The latter was 20ft high and topped with barbed wire. It was patrolled by armed guards who shot any Jews caught outside the ghetto boundary without permission. There were two areas west of the Vistula joined by a footbridge known as the 'Large' and 'Small' ghettos. The former was some three times the size of its southern neighbour. The 'Little Ghetto' was filled with affluent residents and was considered the better place to be.

The Gestapo supervised the Jewish population with the assistance of the Ghetto Police and the Council of Jewish Elders. The two prisons taken over by the Gestapo, the 'Pawiak' and the 'Serbia', were inside the ghetto perimeter. This meant that all those non-Jews who were arrested in Warsaw were sent there for interrogation, torture, execution or shipment to the concentration camps as well.

In October 1940 Hitler's henchmen had decided that Warsaw would be a good place to gather all the Jews rounded up from the occupied territories. At first those housed in the ghetto were free to pass through the gates during the daytime as long as they were wearing a yellow Star of David. Then from 15 October 1941 the gates were sealed and the ghetto effectively became a concentration camp. The following year the forced deportations to the death camps started. By then children living on the streets had begun to die of starvation despite the presence of some well-stocked food shops.

Around 380,000 people from Poland and across Europe were crammed into the ghetto under the administration of the SS-appointed Council of Jewish Elders. Inside communication was a problem, as the Poles spoke Polish or Yiddish so could not easily understand the German, French and Greek Jews. Every day 5,000 were sent to the gas chambers at the Treblinka concentration camp. A Jewish policeman called Szmerling, known as 'the Jewish Torturer', oversaw this process at the Umschlagplatz (Collection Point) rail siding. This was located at the northern edge of the 'Large Ghetto' and was concealed from the rest of the area. The entrance was near the junction of Zamenhoff and Low Streets and led via a maze of pathways to an open square. From there the people were herded onto an old hospital forecourt where they spent the night before being put into cattle trucks in the morning. By early August 1942 around 150,000 Jews had been murdered in this way.

In October 1942 the Germans set up a little-known concentration camp within the city limits known as KZ Warschau. It consisted of five sub-camps linked by railway lines. Two were located in the area of the ghetto and two were near Warsaw's Western station. The fifth served as a transit camp for prisoners of war. The KZ Warschau complex had space for over 41,000 inmates. It included gas chambers. The camps operated until August 1944 by which time up to 200,000 people had died there.

Although conditions in the ghetto were increasingly intolerable, the Jews remained compliant. By 10 September 1942 there were just 30,000 left with another 40,000 in hiding across the city. The Polish Home Army offered to conduct diversionary attacks if there was a Jewish rising. However, the ghetto's leaders felt it best if they cooperated with the Nazis, for fear of the consequences. Few were convinced by such a feeble argument. The younger Jews decided to fight back and created the Undergound Jewish Militant Organisation. The Home Army did what it could to assist smuggling in small quantities of arms and ammunition.

Reichsführer-SS Himmler made a surprise trip to Warsaw in January 1943 to see how the liquidation of the Jews was progressing. When SS-General Friedrich Krueger, the police chief for Cracow, enquired why they had not been notified of the visit he was swiftly put in his place. 'I did not know I was going to Warsaw and I did not inform you!' snapped Himmler in response. By now the remaining Jews were confined to an area just over a square mile. It was evident that at this rate the Jewish presence in the city could not last much longer.

Himmler, convinced his work was almost done, ordered the complete destruction of the Warsaw ghetto by 16 February 1943. In light of commitments elsewhere, especially at Stalingrad, there were not the resources to carry this out. SS-Oberführer von Sammern-Frankenegg was initially put in charge but was relieved by SS-Brigadeführer Jürgen Stroop. He commenced the operation on 19 April. The units involved were largely newly formed and consisted of two reserve SS training battalions, as well as some army cavalry and panzergrenadiers. In all they numbered just over 2,000 men. The SS were reinforced by 335 Lithuanian militia and some Polish police and firemen.

Himmler did not oversee things personally and scurried back to Berlin. Instead he sent Krueger to act as his observer. It was anticipated that this 'special action' would last just three days – in the event it took four weeks. Earlier in the month a Jewish revolt had brought the deportations to a halt. The resistance killed some of the Jewish collaborators and built barricades. These fighters belonged to either the Jewish Military Union or the Jewish Combat Organisation. They then waited for the inevitable German assault. About 600 armed Jews stopped the initial attack but the Germans quickly brought up artillery with which to bombard their positions.

'Hardly had [the] operation begun,' reported Stroop, 'than we ran into strong concerted fire by the Jews and bandits.' A panzer and two armoured cars leading the advance were attacked using Molotov cocktails and forced to retreat. 'About 1730 hours we encountered very strong resistance from one block of buildings, including machine gun fire,' said Stroop. A German assault party stormed the buildings but the Jews slipped away. Stroop's first attack cost him twelve men. On the second night the Red Air Force bombed the city but it did little to help the uprising.

Slowly but surely the defenders were driven back by Stroop's artillery, flamethrowers and tanks. Stroop was baffled why the Jews did not simply give up. During the first phase of his operation it was possible to round up large numbers of Jews, by the second phase it had become much more difficult. As soon as resistance was overcome his forces would encounter another Jewish battle group of twenty to thirty men supported by a similar number of women. The latter fought using pistols and hand grenades.

By day five Himmler was getting increasingly impatient for results. 'I therefore decided,' said Stroop, 'to destroy the entire Jewish area by setting every block on fire.' He hoped this would drive out the Jews but many preferred to remain and perish. His flamethrowers rapidly helped set the ghetto ablaze. Fire was soon threatening the factories that made spare parts and uniforms for the Germans. However, when the Polish fire brigade turned up to try and prevent the fire from spreading they were stopped by the SS. The Jewish fighters trapped in the burning buildings were forced to jump from the upper stories. Those who survived tried to reach the neighbouring blocks, but most were too badly injured or were shot. According to Stroop, the defenders were 'going insane from the heat, the smoke and the explosions'.

Himmler was informed on 25 April that 27,464 Jews had been captured. Many were sent to Treblinka. The following day Stroop signalled to Himmler to report that his forces had killed 362 Jews in battle and shot another 1,330. Just 30 prisoners were taken. In early May the Germans rounded up Maximilian Lichtenbaum, Sherishevsky, Alfred Stegman and Gustav Tselikovsky, all members of the Jewish Council and executed them. The Community Chairman Chernyakov took his own life. In London Shmul Zigelbaum, a member of the National Council of the Polish Government in Exile, also committed suicide to draw attention to the terrible plight of the ghetto. The fighting continued. Stroop even resorted to flooding the sewers in an effort to flush out the remaining Jews. His men also dropped smoke bombs down the manholes.

Jewish resistance was finally stamped out on 16 May 1943. 'One hundred and eight Jews, bandits and subhumans were destroyed,' reported Stroop that day. 'The former Jewish quarter of Warsaw is no longer in existence.' At 2015 hours his men blew up the Warsaw synagogue.

According to Stroop, some 56,065 Jews were killed or captured. This included 7,000 killed in the ghetto and 6,929 sent to Treblinka. A further 6,000 perished in the flames of the burning ghetto. This left around 36,000 unaccounted for but it was assumed they had gone to the gas chambers. Stoop claimed he had lost 16 dead and 90 wounded, but this seems suspiciously low.

Stroop, who had been serving as the higher police leader in Greece, treated the destruction of the ghetto as if it were a military campaign rather than a police operation. His seventy-five-page report and photographs were bound as an album called *The Warsaw Ghetto is No More!* and presented to Himmler. The latter used this to convince Hitler that the Jews had built strongpoints in the ghetto and that the SS had fought a real battle. Stroop said the conduct of his men had been 'exemplary'. Warsaw's agony, though, was far from over.

In the wake of the destruction of the ghetto the Home Army stepped up its attacks on the occupiers. A casino frequented by German officers was blown up. The Gestapo and German police were attacked on the streets. Five insurgents gunned down SS-Oberscharführer Franz Bürkl, the deputy commander of Pawiak Prison, on 7 September 1943. He and several colleagues were killed near the Gestapo headquarters in Szuch Avenue. His Alsatian dog, which had been trained to attack prisoners, was also shot. In the western Praga district fuel supplies for the German armed forces were set alight. Then on 8 October the Home Army blew up all the railway lines leading out of the city. This paralysed supplies being sent to the Eastern Front.

The ghetto in Warsaw was not the only one as the Germans established them elsewhere. Most notably at Lodz where up to 250,000 Jews were gathered. In September 1942 17,000 people were removed from there and killed. In December of that year another 25,000 suffered the same fate. There were just 74,000 Jews left by 1 January 1944. Himmler gave the order to liquidate the Lodz ghetto on 10 June 1944. By the time the Red Army arrived there were just 850 people left.

SS-Brigadeführer Stroop's operation against the Warsaw ghetto commenced on 19 April 1943. Although an SS policing operation, it was conducted with military precision.

During the initially stages Stroop's men were able to round up large numbers of Jews without too much opposition.

German troops overseeing the evacuation of civilians in the Umschlagplatz area.

German officers discussing the evacuation of a factory, 24 April 1943. The soldier on the left with the submachine gun is Josef Blösche. The Jews called him 'Frankenstein' thanks to his monstrous behaviour in the ghetto where he committed rape and murder.

More civilians coming out of a large building under the watchful eye of German security forces.

On 25 April 1943 Stroop informed Reichsführer-SS Himmler that 27,464 Jews had been successfully rounded up.

Above and below: Radio operators receiving orders from the back of staff car. The Jews had to rely on runners to communicate between the various groups.

German artillery in Zamenhofa Street shelling a Jewish 'stronghold'.

The gun crew
watches as the
building straight-
ahead collapses.

Once resistance started to increase, Stroop decided to set fire to the ghetto in order to flush out the Jewish fighters.

SS soldiers watching the fires on Nowolipie Street. The flames forced many trapped Jewish fighters to jump, resulting in death or serious injury.

Opposite above: A Jewish fighter plumets to his death as he tries to escape a blazing building in Niska Street.

Opposite below: Relaxed-looking SS soldiers moving along Nowolipie Street.

SS troops take a break during the wanton destruction of the Warsaw ghetto. They treated it as a military, rather than police, operation, which was hard to justify in light of the numbers of civilians involved.

Above: Stroop in the centre with his adjutant watches as the ghetto burns. The smiles on the faces of the soldiers makes the situation seem even more callous.

Opposite above: A Jewish fighter emerges from his bunker on 9 May 1943. He faced almost certain death.

Opposite below: Stroop hosted SS-Obergruppenfürer Maximillian von Herf on 14 May 1944, seen here questioning some locals.

This famous photograph came to epitomise the tragedy of the Warsaw ghetto. The expression on the young boy's face says it all. The man holding the submachine gun was later identified as Josef Blösche – aka 'Frankenstein'.

The last of the Jewish fighters being rounded up. Resistance continued until 16 May 1943, and on that day Stroop reported that his men had killed 108 Jews.

Jews being taken to the Umschlagplatz. According to Stroop, a total of 56,065 Jews were killed or captured.

The ghetto continues to burn. The Germans deliberately stopped the Polish fire brigade from preventing the flames spreading to other parts of Warsaw.

Opposite: A German Maxim machine-gun crew stand on guard at an intersection of Nowolipie and Smocza streets. There was no escape for Warsaw's Jews.

Marching off to their deaths. On 16 May 1943 Stroop signalled, 'The former Jewish quarter of Warsaw is no longer in existence.'

Chapter Five

The Second Battle for Warsaw

In Moscow Stalin knew that to safeguard the Soviet Union in the future he would need to carve out a massive security buffer in Eastern Europe. To do this as a minimum he wanted to establish communist governments in Poland, Hungary, Romania and Bulgaria. He knew that if the Red Army took Berlin, then eastern Germany would become communist as well. Poland presented a potential problem because unlike the others it was not a Germany ally.

Although Stalin had brutally beheaded those Polish forces captured in eastern Poland in 1939, if he was to install a pro-Soviet government in Warsaw he needed to cultivate friendly forces. To achieve this, he turned to the thousands of Polish prisoners and exiles in the Soviet Union. Stalin's first attempt failed. The army of General Wladyslaw Anders managed to slip his grasp in 1942 by getting redeployed to fight with the British in the Middle East and Italy.

A second Polish army was formed in the Soviet Union as the military wing of the so-called Union of Polish Patriots, which came into being with Stalin's approval in 1943. General Zygmunt Berling's Soviet-trained Polish 1st Army finally joined Marshal Rokossovsky's 1st Byelorussian Front during the spring of 1944. Berling had 104,000 men under arms, comprising 5 infantry divisions, a tank brigade, 4 artillery brigades and an air wing. Many recruits who were former prisoners of war saw it as a way of getting home, though Stalin kept them on a tight political leash. For his plans to work it was important that Berling liberated Warsaw and no one else.

In the summer of 1944 the Red Army launched Operation Bagration which smashed Hitler's Army Group Centre in spectacular fashion. Rokossovsky's Lublin-Brest Offensive was conducted from 18 July–2 August 1944 as a follow up to Bagration and to support Konev's Lvov-Sandomierz offensive by tying down German forces in central-eastern Poland and culminated in the Battle of Radzymin.

To the north of Konev's 1st Ukrainian Front, Rokossovsky's 8th Guards, 47th and 69th armies supported by the 2nd Tank Army and the Polish 1st Army struck from the Kovel area towards Lublin and Warsaw, thereby making Army Group North Ukraine's position untenable.

Berling was instructed to cross at Pulawy on 31 July on a wide front in order to support other elements of the Soviet 69th and 8th Guards armies crossing near

Magnuszew. The Polish 1st and 2nd Infantry divisions gained the west bank on 1 and 2 August, but by the 4th had suffered 1,000 casualties and were ordered to withdraw. They were then assigned to protect the northern part of the Magnuszew bridgehead.

In five weeks of fighting Rokossovsky covered 453 miles and was within reach of Warsaw. The Polish capital looked a tempting prize as a culmination of Bagration's remarkable success, but Stalin's summer offensive was beginning to lose momentum. Rokossovsky's 1st Byelorussian Front was at the very limit of its supply lines; ammunition and rations were exhausted, as were his men.

In many ways the German defence of Warsaw echoed that of Minsk, the eastern approaches of the Polish capital were protected by a 50-mile ring of strongpoints. The only difference was that this time Field Marshal Model had sufficient mobile reserves with which to parry Rokossovsky's thrusts. He had gathered his wits and more importantly sufficient men with which to thwart Rokossovsky's oncoming tide.

By this stage the German defences were coalescing around 5 weak panzer divisions deploying around 450 tanks and self-propelled guns. Over the next week things would start to go badly wrong for Rokossovsky and his front would experience its first major setback.

North of Warsaw Model turned to Reichsführer-SS Himmler's Waffen-SS for assistance in stabilising the front. The remnants of the 1st SS and 2nd SS Panzer divisions had been shipped west after their mauling in the Kamenets-Podolsk Pocket to re-equip and prepare for the anticipated Anglo-American landings in France. However, the 3rd SS and 5th SS Panzer divisions remained in Romania and Poland rearming.

The 3rd SS was notified to move north as early as 25 June, but the disruption to the rail networks and roads meant that it took two weeks to get to northeastern Poland. Arriving on 7 July, it found the Red Amy was already striking towards the Polish city of Grodno and threatening the southern flank of Army Group Centre's Fourth Army and the northern flank of Second Army.

Deployed to Grodno, the 3rd SS was assigned the task of creating a defensive line for Fourth Army to retire behind. Spectacularly the division held off 400 Soviet tanks for 11 days before withdrawing southwest towards Warsaw. Joined by the Hermann Göring Panzer Division at Siedlce, 50 miles east of the Polish capital, they held the Soviets for almost a week from 24 July, keeping open an escape corridor for Second Army as it fled towards the Vistula. Three days later the Soviets threw almost 500 tanks to the south and by the 29th were at the suburbs of Warsaw.

The 5th SS arrived in western Warsaw on 27 July and trundled through the city to take up positions to the east. The next day Stalin ordered Rokossovsky to occupy Praga, Warsaw's suburbs on the eastern bank of the Vistula, during 5–8 August and to establish a number of bridgeheads over the river to the south of the city.

Rokossovsky at this stage enjoyed a three to one superiority in infantry and five to one in armour and artillery. His front had at its disposal 9 armies: 1 tank army, 2 tank corps, 3 cavalry corps, 1 motorised corps and 2 air armies. Against this Model's Second Army could muster 4 understrength panzer divisions and 1 infantry division, while Ninth Army had just 2 divisions and 2 brigades of infantry.

The Soviet 2nd Tank Army and 8th Tank Corps attacked westwards along the Warsaw–Lublin road toward Praga. About 40 miles southeast of Warsaw in the Garwolin area 2nd Tank was opposed by two advanced battalions, of Generalleutnant Dr Fritz Franek's 10,800-strong German 73rd Infantry Division. Holding the north bank of the Swidra River, they were backed up by the Hermann Göring Panzer Division 12 miles east of Praga.

In addition four panzer divisions, the 3rd SS, 5th SS, 4th and 19th, poised to counterattack, now defended the approaches to Warsaw. The men of the 19th Panzer Division were veterans of the Eastern Front having fought on the central and southern sectors from June 1941 to June 1944, before being shipped to the Netherlands for a refit.

When the 2nd Tank Army's 16th Tank Corps struck toward Otwock along the Lublin road the 19th Panzer counterattacked with forty panzers and an infantry regiment. However, it was unable to hold Otwock and by the evening the Soviets were a mere 15 miles from Warsaw having taken the villages near Milosna Stara. They were now poised to assault the key defences of Okuniew. The 8th Tank Corps opened the attack only to be stalled by determined German air and artillery attack.

In the meantime, Vedeneev's 3rd Corps bypassed German positions in the Zielonka district and drove them from Wolomin (also spelt Volomin) and Radzymin, just 12 and 16 miles northeast of Warsaw where they took up defensive positions along the Dluga River. Having outstretched his supply lines and outrun the rest of the Soviet 2nd Tank Army, Vedeneev was in a dangerously exposed position. The XXXIX Panzer Corps was in the area and five German panzer divisions were coming together in the direction of Radzymin–Wolomin.

Rokossovsky's forces were quick to react to this threat and attempted to alleviate the pressure on Vedeneev's 3rd Tank Corps with a diversionary attack. At dawn on 31 July, followed by heavy air and artillery bombardment, the Soviet 8th Tank Corps threw themselves at the Germans who fell back toward Okuniew. The 5th SS counterattacked in a westerly direction with fifty panzers from Stanislawow in an effort to link up with the Hermann Göring and 19th Panzer divisions which were fighting tank battles with the Soviets at Okuniew and Ossow.

The 5th SS were repulsed and on the evening of the 31st the Soviets took Okuniew, but could not budge the Germans from their strongpoint at Ossow. North of the Soviet 8th Tank Corps, the 3rd Tank remained unsupported and like the 16th Corps had endured a day of heavy attacks from German armour, artillery and infantry. The commander of the Soviet 2nd Army was in an impossible position – his units were suffering heavy casualties, he was short of supplies and his rear was under threat.

Model began to probe the weak spot in Rokossovsky's line between Praga and Siedlce. His intention was to hit the Soviets in the flank and the rear and soon to the northeast of Warsaw the XXXIX Panzer Corps was counterattacking the 3rd Tank Corps and driving it back to Wolomin.

The 3rd SS, Hermann Göring and 4th and 19th Panzer divisions struck south into the unsupported Soviet columns. The Hermann Göring 1st Armoured Paratroop Regiment launched the counterattack from Praga toward Wolomin on the 31st, heralding a much larger effort to halt the Red Army before Warsaw. While from the southwest along the Warsaw–Wyszków road attacking towards Radzymin came the 19th Panzer. From Wyszków 4th Panzer acted in support.

The next day from Wegrow pushing towards Wolomin came the 5th SS. At the same time the 3rd SS was launched into the fray from Siedlce towards Stanislawow with the intention of trapping those Soviet forces on the northeastern bank of the Dluga.

Rokossovsky simply could not fulfil his orders to break though the German defences and enter Praga by 8 August – it was impossible. On 1 August at 1610 hours he ordered the attack to be broken off just as Model launched his major counterattack.

General Nikolaus von Vormann, appointed by Guderian to command the Ninth Army, bringing up reinforcements from Second Army's reserves also launched a counterattack. Using units of the 5th SS and 3rd SS attacking from the forests to the east of Michalow, he drove the Soviet 8th Tank Corps from Okuniew at 2100 hours on 1 August and linked up with XXXIX Panzer Corps from the west.

On 2 August all Soviet forces assaulting Warsaw were redirected. The 28th, 47th and 65th armies were instructed northwards to seize the undefended town of Wyszków and the Liwiec River line. Crucially this left the 2nd Tank Army without infantry support. This situation was compounded when the 69th Army was ordered to halt while the 8th Guards Army under Vasily Chuikov ceased the assault to await a German attack from the direction of Garwolin.

By the 2nd the 19th followed by 4th Panzer were in Radzymin, northeast of Warsaw and the Soviet 3rd Tank Corps was thrown back towards Wolomin. The following day the Hermann Göring Panzer Division rolled into Wolomin. Pressed into the area of Wolomin, Vedeneev's 3rd Tank Corps was trapped. Attempts by the 8th Guards Tank Corps and the 16th Tank Corps to reach them failed, with the 8th Guards suffering serious casualties in the attempt.

After a week of heavy fighting the Soviet 3rd Tank Corps was surrounded by 4th and 19th Panzer divisions, and 3,000 Soviet troops had been killed and another

6,000 captured. The Soviets also lost 425 of the 808 tanks and self-propelled guns they had begun the battle with on 18 July. By noon on 5 August the Germans had ceased their counterattack and the battle for the Praga approaches had come to an end. Two German divisions had to be transferred south to deal with the Soviet threat there.

The 3rd Tank Corps was destroyed and the 8th Guards Tank Corps and the 16th Tank Corps had taken major losses. The exhausted Soviet 2nd Tank Army handed over it positions to the 47th and 70th armies and withdrew to lick its wounds. Post-war communist propagandists cited the Battle of Radzymin as evidence that the German counterattack prevented the Red Army from helping the Warsaw uprising.

Stalin clearly did not hold Lieutenant General Vedeneev responsible for the encirclement and destruction of his command. He remained in charge and the 3rd Tank Corps was honoured by being designated the 9th Guards Tank Corps in November 1944.

It was not until 25 August that Rokossovsky would inform Stalin that he was ready to have another go at Warsaw. After such heavy fighting northeast of the Polish capital it is easy to see why Stalin saw the Polish Home Army's Warsaw rising of little consequence in the overall strategic scheme of things.

Great areas of central Warsaw were left in ruins after the Warsaw ghetto rising was crushed.

The Germans discovered that Jewish fighters had built hidden bunkers in the cellars of the ghetto.

The secret Jewish bunkers even included stoves.

This was the image that the Germans liked to portray in occupied Poland, Ukraine and Byelorussia – fraternal friendship. It was a propaganda lie.

Field Marshal von Busch (centre) with Field Marshal von Rundstedt (on the left), who was appointed commander of Army Group Centre in October 1943.

A German MG 34 team in Russia. By mid-1944 Hitler's army groups were stretched thin on the Eastern Front and were short of manpower and tanks.

At 0500 hours on 23 June 1944 Stalin launched Operation Bagration, his version of D-Day which was to liberate Minsk and Byelorussia. His tank armies included the new upgunned T-34/85.

Field Marshal von Busch's Army Group Centre had hardly any tanks and within a week was sent reeling. Von Busch, on the left, clearly looks unhappy about the latest reports.

By early July Stalin's tank columns were in Minsk, and by the end of the month they were approaching Warsaw and the Vistula.

Army Group Centre lost 55,000 men killed and wounded in the Minsk area alone during 5–11 July 1944.

Knocked out Panzer IVs belonging to the 20th Panzer Division. When Operation Bagration sliced through Army Group Centre 20th Panzer was sent to try and stem the tide.

German transport on the Eastern Front, note the use of buses. Bagration shattered Army Group Centre's divisions and sent the Germans into headlong retreat towards Poland.

During June and July 1944 Hitler's Wehrmacht suffered over 620,000 casualties, half of which were lost by Army Group Centre.

Bagration cost the Red Army 168,000 casualties.

German anti-tank guns captured by the Red Army. Army Group Centre lost most of its heavy equipment.

German transport, comprising buses, lorries, staff cars and radio trucks, abandoned during the summer of 1944.

Soviet and Polish troops in the Lithuanian capital Vilnius in July 1944. The Soviet-raised Polish 1st Army was to play a key role in the liberation of Warsaw.

This Panther tank belonged to the 5th SS Panzer Division *Wiking*. Operation Bagration took the Red Army to the very gates of Warsaw. Himmler's tough Waffen-SS managed to bring the Soviet advance to a halt before it could liberate the city.

Himmler had no military experience but was served by highly competent generals. He saw the defence of Warsaw as yet another way for his Waffen-SS to gain favour with Hitler.

Destroyed Panthers, which look like they were attempting an all-round defence. A massive tank battle to the east of Warsaw at Radzymin in early August 1944 witnessed a Red Army defeat.

The 5th SS and 3rd SS caught the Soviet 8th Tank Corps at Okuniew. Subsequently it and the 16th Tank Corps suffered heavy casualties and the 3rd Tank Corps was destroyed.

A Tiger from the 3rd SS Panzer Division *Totenkopf*. This division was also involved in rebuffing the Red Army east of Warsaw.

SS-Panzergrenadiers watch clouds of smoke rising on the horizon. The Red Army was stalled before Warsaw and the city would not be liberated until January 1945.

Another 5th SS Panther on the open killing grounds east of Warsaw.

A *Totenkopf* Panzer IV emerging from some woods. The crew are wearing a mixture of uniforms.

Tough-looking Soviet tankers. In the space of two weeks the Red Army lost 425 tanks and self-propelled guns in the fighting near Warsaw.

During the Lvov–Sandomierz Offensive the Red Army suffered a further 198,000 casualties. Stalin viewed this as a small price to pay for the annihilation of Army Group Centre and the mauling of Army Groups North and North Ukraine. It also put Warsaw firmly in his grasp.

Chapter Six

Warsaw Rising

Operation Big Scheme was the Polish resistance's plan for a national uprising, to coincide with the arrival of Stalin's forces. The revolt, codenamed Burza or Tempest, was to start in eastern Poland where the Polish Home Army's 3rd, 9th and 27th divisions would attempt to wrest control from the Germans ahead of the advancing Red Army. This would force the latter to recognise the Home Army's authority in the liberated areas.

The rising commenced in January 1944 when the 6,000-strong 27th Division fought the Germans and the Ukrainian Insurgent Army for control of the Wołyn area. Contact with the Red Army was first made that March in Wołyn. This, though, did not help the Poles' cause. By June 1944 the Germans had surrounded the 27th Division, the survivors managing to escape to the Lublin area. However, they were taken prisoner by the Soviets and shipped East.

Lieutenant General Tadeusz Bór-Komorowski, commander of the Home Army, knew that securing Warsaw was the key to the success of the uprising. If they liberated the capital this would prevent Stalin having a say on the composition of Poland's future government. The German armed forces were in complete disarray and it seemed unlikely that they would try and hold the city for long. The rising in Warsaw would start in anticipation of the Red Army crossing the Vistula River after the spectacular success of Stalin's Operation Bagration.

At Cracow, the capital of the German General Government, the Wehrmacht garrison was 30,000 strong, twice that of Warsaw which had a much bigger population. In addition there were some 10,000 armed German administrators in the city. As a result it was decided that there would be no secondary Home Army rising in Cracow.

By the end of July, with the Eastern Front having all but collapsed, the time looked ripe for the Poles to act. At that point the Germans instructed 100,000 residents of Warsaw to make themselves available to work on the city's defences. The Poles boycotted the order. Partly in response to this, the Germans began evacuating their administrative personnel.

On 1 August at Magnuszew, just 12½ miles south of Warsaw, Chuikov's 8th Guards Army crossed the Vistula. He held onto his tiny bridgehead despite determined counterattacks by the 9th Panzer, Hermann Göring and 45th Grenadier divisions. If he had turned north, he could have fought his way to Praga.

That day Bór-Komorowski ordered his men to rise up against the German occupation of Warsaw at 1700 hours. Poor communications meant that orders were staggered with the subsector commanders being informed at 0800 hours, the district commanders 2 hours later and the unit commanders at midday. Platoon commanders did not get their orders until 1400 hours. This caused delay and confusion resulting in only about a third of their weapons being issued.

Bór-Komorowski, hurrying to his headquarters in the Kamler tobacco factory, observed on the streets:

> Overcoats bulged with hand grenades, or did not quite conceal from my eyes a tommy gun or a rifle. Though I knew that only a person in the street would notice these things, I could not repress an irrational anxiety. I passed German patrols at every few paces, and armoured cars were moving ceaselessly through the streets.

Fighting soon broke out prematurely. In Wilson Square in the northern suburb of Zoliborz the Poles opened fire on German police. The latter called in reinforcements and after a 3-hour battle the Poles were defeated. The violence spread to the Czerniakow district, Napoleon Square, Kercely Square, Mirowski Square and Chochim Street in the Wola area near Bór-Komorowski's headquarters.

Colonel Geibel, commander of the SS and police in the city, at 1600 hours received intelligence from a Luftwaffe officer that a general rising was schedule for 1700 hours. Geibel immediately notified Lieutenant General Reiner Stahel, the garrison commander, who put all German forces on alert. Within an hour Stahel's headquarters in the Brühl Palace came under attack.

At his headquarters Bór-Komorowski was waiting for his forces to gather prior to attacking a nearby German unit protected by two pillboxes. Unfortunately, one of his sentries shot at a passing German vehicle before he was ready. Superior numbers of Germans launched an attack on his position. It looked as if it would be overwhelmed when suddenly the city erupted into open revolt and reinforcements arrived in the nick of time.

Just after 1800 hours Bór-Komorowski was summoned to the roof to see the Polish flag flying defiantly from the sixteen-storey Prudential building that dominated the city centre. Looking around, he saw others fluttering over the Town Hall, the Post Office Savings Bank and many more. This was the first time the Polish flag had been raised over the city since 1939. Barricades went up across the city and members of the Home Army sought to secure all the city's public utility works.

However, at the telephone exchange the Germans barricaded themselves inside and refused to budge.

The Germans had not been taken by complete surprise. Crucially they held the airport, the police and army headquarters, the radio station and the Vistula bridges. Stahel and his commanders were hampered though as they had no contingency plans or the manpower to deal with such a widespread rising. In consequence for the first few days their response was ill-coordinated.

Governor Frank, at his headquarters in Cracow, was alarmed by Stahel's report early in the evening of 1 August. Frank's strong garrison was put on alert in case they were subjected to similar attacks. His main concern though was for the German Ninth Army's supply routes through Warsaw over the Vistula to the battlefields to the east of Praga. General Wilhelm Koppe, the SS Police chief, also in Cracow, telephoned Geibel to inform him that reinforcements were on their way. When Stahel learned of this he decided to go on to the defensive until this help arrived.

Rokossovsky, who was ordered to go over to the defensive, watched the Germans systemically crush the insurrection for two whole months. Likewise, the Red Air Force, which was just 100 miles, away did very little. On the morning of 2 August Rokossovsky went to view the Polish capital and got a good indication of the Polish Home Army's efforts, recalling:

> Together with a group of officers I was visiting the 2nd Tank Army, which was fighting on that sector of the front. From our observation point, which had been set up at the top of a tall factory chimney, we could see Warsaw. The city was covered in clouds of smoke. Here and there houses were burning. Bombs and shells were exploding. Everything indicated that a battle was in progress.

By 4 August 1944 the Polish Home Army had secured most of central Warsaw, but lacking heavy weapons and ammunition it was unable to consolidate its half-dozen defensive enclaves within the city. The first major German counterattack occurred two days later in the vicinity of Chlodna Street in the Gryybów district to the west of the Vistula. The Germans counterattacked again on 10 August and four days later the Home Army had been firmly divided into six enclaves.

In the meantime the Red Army stood by. By the end of the first week of August its Magnuszew bridgehead contained the Soviet 4th, 28th and 29th Guards Rifle corps. Holding the northern shoulder of the bridgehead preventing the Soviets from expanding it was the 1132nd Volskgrenadier Brigade and the Panzer Abteilung 902, while to the south were the 17th Infantry Division.

Why did Rokossovsky not try for a bridgehead at Warsaw if the Red Army had established footholds at Magnuszew, Pulawy and on the upper Vistula near

Sandomierz? To have done so would have been far tougher than in the Radom region way to the south, Sandomierz had cost them dearly. Furthermore the Soviets saw Warsaw anchoring the Germans' defensive line on the Narev and Bobr and in turn East Prussia and knew they would fight bitterly to defend this. Without the Baltic States secured Hitler could strike from East Prussia against the flank and rear of the Red Army once it was advancing beyond the Vistula.

Also by now Rokossovsky was facing twenty-two German divisions. These included four security divisions in the Warsaw suburbs, three Hungarian divisions on the Vistula south of Warsaw and the remains of six or seven divisions that had escaped from the chaos of Belostok and Brest-Litovsk. They could be deployed between the Narev and the Western Bug. At least eight divisions were identified fighting to the north of Siedlce, among them two panzer and three SS panzer or panzergrenadier divisions. In reality, regardless of the military situation, Stalin was waiting in the wings with his own Polish government and armed forces.

Marshal Zhukov blamed Bór-Komorowski for a lack of cooperation with the Red Army:

As was established later, neither the command of the Front [Rokossovsky] nor that of Poland's 1st Army [Berling] had been informed in advance by Bór-Komorowski, the leader of the uprising, about forthcoming events in Warsaw. Nor did he make any attempt to coordinate the insurgents' actions with those of the 1st Byelorussian Front. The Soviet Command learned about the uprising after the event from local residents who had crossed the Vistula. The Stavka had not been informed in advance either.

On instructions by the Supreme Commander, two paratroop officers were sent to Bór-Komorowski for liaison and coordination of actions. However, Bór-Komorowski refused to receive the officers. . . .

I have ascertained that our troops did everything they possibly could to help the insurgents, although the uprising had not been in anyway coordinated with the Soviet command.

In light of Rokossovsky's efforts to the northeast and southeast of Warsaw in the face of the tough Waffen-SS this is largely true. Meanwhile, the Germans prepared to crush the Polish Home Army.

General Tadeusz Bór-Komorowski, commander of the Polish Home Army or *Armia Krajowa*. Bór (meaning 'The Forest') was actually his wartime codename. During the First World War he had fought as an officer with the Austro-Hungarian Army. On 1 August 1944 he ordered his men and women to rise up in Warsaw in anticipation of the arrival of the Red Army.

Members of the Home Army openly carrying weapons and making their way through the streets, 1 August 1944. Zero hour was timed for 1700 hours but things did not go according to plan.

Polish fighters defending a barricade. Unfortunately, the uprising orders to the various Polish commands in Warsaw were staggered. This resulted in the rising starting before schedule and before all the weapons could be issued.

The central fighter is armed with the Polish Blyskawica (lightning) submachine gun. This was modelled on the German MP40 and the British Sten and massproduced for the Home Army. Fighting first erupted in the district of Zoliborz. The Germans took 3 hours to subdue the insurgents but by then the violence had spread across the city.

A young Polish nurse in Muranowska Street. The poster on the door is a call to arms for the *Armia Krajowa*.

Some of the German-occupied buildings were protected by concrete bunkers or pillboxes. The area around Bór-Komorowski's headquarters in the Kamler tobacco factory became a battleground when his plans for attacking two pillboxes were carried out prematurely by his men.

The Home Army wore whatever uniforms they could lay their hands on. They were critically short of heavy weapons and largely had to rely on rifles and submachine guns. Many units did not have enough weapons to go round, so unarmed fighters had to wait until armed comrades were either killed or wounded.

Home Army soldiers wearing some semblance of a regular uniform.

The Home Army ranks included women fighters.

Very young Home Army fighters in Warsaw, 2 September 1944. They belonged to the Moitła Battalion which formed part of the Radoslaw Regiment. At this stage there was still an air of optimism.

A burnt-out German Panzer IV on the streets of Warsaw. The Home Army had very few anti-tank weapons or mines, so had in many instances to rely on Molotov cocktails.

Concentration camp prisoners liberated by the Home Army.

Polish fighters with a captured German Sd Kfz 251 half-track. This particular vehicle belonged to the panzergrenadiers of the 5th SS Panzer Division *Wiking* and was taken on 14 August 1944. Dubbed 'Gray Wolf', it was used in an attack on German troops holding the central campus of Warsaw University. The Home Army ended up with a few enemy half-tracks, tanks and a scratch-built armoured car.

The Home Army made use of several captured Panther tanks. This one was deployed on the junction of Okopowa Street and Wolność Street.

The Polish Panthers were operated by the Wacek Tank Platoon in support of the Zośka Battalion. While a welcome addition to the Home Army's meagre armoury, they did not last very long.

A Polish soldier firing the Blyskawica submachine gun. This was ideal for the close-quarter combat in Warsaw.

The Poles blocked the approaches to the Vistula bridges in Warsaw, including the Kierbedź Bridge. Built in the 1860s, this bridge connected the Old Town with Praga.

Chapter Seven

Tragic Last Stand

In response to the Polish Home Army's uprising the Germans rapidly despatched reinforcements to Warsaw. In August 1944 General Reiner Stahel's 12,000-strong garrison comprised 5,000 regular troops, 4,000 Luftwaffe personnel (over a quarter of whom were manning the air defences) and a 2,000-strong security regiment. Wehrmacht forces in the immediate area numbered up to 16,000 men, with another 90,000 further afield.

With the Wehrmacht fully tied up fending off the Red Army, it was left to the SS to crush the Polish rising. SS-Standartenführer Paul Geibel's police and SS units totalled 5,710 men, supported by 3,500 factory and rail guards. Geibel also managed to scrounge four Tiger tanks, a Panther tank, four other medium tanks and an assault gun from the 5th SS Panzer Division *Wiking* to strengthen his command.

Army Group Centre was to have a limited role in fighting. General Vormann, commanding the Ninth Army, sent 1,000 East Prussian Grenadiers to Praga to help hold the Poniatowski Bridge on 3 August. An additional three battalions were also sent to help to assist the Hermann Göring Regiment clearing a way through the city to the Kierbedź Bridge.

On Himmler's express orders a motley battle group of around 12,000 troops under SS-Gruppenführer Heinz Reinefarth was swiftly assembled to help Geibel deal with the insurgents. These reinforcements included SS-Brigadeführer Bronislav Kaminski's Russian National Liberation Army Brigade (*Russkaia Osvoboditelnania Norodnaia Armiia* – RONA), numbering 1,585 Cossacks and Ukrainians. Kaminski supported SS-Oberführer Oskar Dirlewanger's larger anti-partisan brigade some 3,381 strong. This consisted of 2 battalions of 865 released criminals, 3 battalions of former Soviet prisoners of war, 2 companies of gendarmes, a police platoon and an artillery battery. They all headed for Warsaw on 3 August.

The following day Himmler flew to Poznan from his headquarters in East Prussia, and gathered some 8,000 men under Reinefarth supported by 37 assault guns, a company of heavy tanks, 4 heavy mortars and 150 flamethrowers. Additionally, Colonel Wilhelm Schmidt supplied 2,000 men drawn from the 603rd Regiment as well as a grenadier and police battalion. They were also supported by artillery, 15 heavy mortars and 8 flamethrowers.

All the German forces in Warsaw were placed under SS-Obergruppenführer Erich von dem Bach-Zelewski during the first week of August. A specialist in anti-partisan operations, he had been overseeing the construction of defences on the Vistula near Gdansk. Bach-Zelewski was soon to discover both Kaminski and Dirlewanger's militias were ill-disciplined.

Bach-Zelewski thought the Kaminski Brigade was the lowest of the low, remarking, 'The fighting value of these Cossacks was, as usual in such a collection of people without a fatherland, very poor. They had a great liking for alcohol and other excesses and had no interest in military discipline.' In contrast, he noted, 'Dirlewanger's brigade possessed the highest fighting qualities.'

Reinefarth's first detachments reached the western suburbs of Wola on 4 August. When he visited Vormann's headquarters, at Skierniewicz, 45 miles southwest of the city, he learned that the Poles were blocking the approaches to the Vistula bridges. In response the Germans had constructed two pontoon bridges, one to the south at Siekierki and the other to the north at Bielany. The Poles controlled the Old Town and part of Mokotow. They had also captured the Post Office station astride the Warsaw railway and blocked the line. Previously every 24 hours on average fifty German military supply trains had passed through the city heading east. Now none were getting through.

Despite being pounded by the Luftwaffe, the Poles controlled all the main highway crossroads. This meant that any time the garrison tried to move anywhere they came under fire and suffered heavy losses. In the ghetto ruins German positions were being shelled by a homemade self-propelled gun, comprising a lorry carrying a field gun. From the Germans' perspective the only good news was that the resistance had been subdued in Praga.

Vormann explained that his Ninth Army was concentrating all its efforts in containing the Red Army at Magnuszew, south of Warsaw. Reinefarth's job was to attack east from Wola along a line Chlodna, Saxon Gardens and the Brühl Palace in order to relieve General Stahel. General Rohr, the previous garrison commandant, with another group was also to fight east up Jerusalem Avenue towards the Vistula. In all they were to commit about 7,300 men.

During the night the Home Army, aided by local people, strengthened their barricades and dug anti-tank ditches. Some supplies dropped by the RAF reached them in Wola. The Home Army, numbering about 4,000 fighters, was warned about the German reinforcements so knew it was outnumbered three to one.

Just after dawn on 5 August German bombers, without fighter cover, dropped high explosives and incendiaries onto the Wola district. This forced the civilian population towards the city centre. German troops then counterattacked. Dirlewanger and

Schmidt's men advanced behind tanks along Wolska and Gorzewska streets heading for Kercely Square. The tanks blasted the Poles' barricades at close range, then the infantry stepped forward with their flamethrowers. Kaminski's Cossacks struck along Grojecka Street towards Narutowizc Square, to try and seize the area south of Wola. In response Colonel Radóslaw reinforced his defences with two battalions and two captured German tanks. The latter drove into the ghetto and set free 350 Jews held in the concentration camp.

The following morning on 6 August the Luftwaffe returned with its bombers and fighter-bombers attacking the barricades on the Chlodna–Towarowa crossroads and Kercely Square. Dirlewanger's brigade was soon pushing along Chlodna and Elektoralna streets towards Theatre Square and the Brühl Palace. This drove a wedge through Polish resistance in Wola to the city centre.

The Poles, short of weapons and running out of ammunition, had little choice but to fall back to the Palace of Justice in Leszno. Once the Germans had overwhelmed the defences in Chlodna and Ogrodowa streets the Poles had to retreat even further towards the city centre. By midday Dirlewanger's men had reached the Saxon Gardens and Theatre Square. Contact was then made with the SS units holding Brühl Palace. They were just in time as General Stahel's men were on the point of giving up.

Dirlewanger, supported by two Tiger tanks and a Poznan police battalion, renewed the onslaught on 7 August. The Poles were forced back along Elektoralna. The Germans also pushed along Leszno Street. Kaminski's brigade made faltering progress from Ochtoa toward the city centre. In truth he and his men were more interested in the contents of the Machorka factory – namely vodka. The Poles launched a counterattack towards Wola but were met by a Panther tank and several armoured cars.

By 2000 hours the Germans had secured the Wolska–Chlodna–Elektoralna–Saxon Gardens artery. They had almost reached the Kierbedź Bridge. An appalling massacre took place in Elektoralna Street carried out by Dirlewanger and Kaminski's men. At the Marie Curie Radium Institute on 5 August drunken Cossacks took part in atrocities against the civilian staff and patients. Rape and murder was followed by the hospital being set on fire.

For two days they ran amok in Wola, the western part of the city centre and Ochota. Atrocities also took place at St Lazarus' Hospital and Wola Hospital. At the Ursus factory civilians were herded into the yard and shot. It was estimated that up to 7,000 people were murdered there. After the war the German officers involved disingenuously laid the blame firmly on Kaminski and Dirlewanger. They, however, were in command. Between 5 and 7 August almost 40,000 civilians were executed or lost to the flames.

'They gave no mercy in battle and did not expect any,' said von dem Bach-Zelewski of Direlwanger's brigade. 'As a result they suffered losses three times as great as those of any other German unit . . .'. He thought little of Reinefarth's Poznan police group in the attack, but noted they were good in the defence and much better disciplined than Dirlewanger's men. He was also impressed by Colonel Schmidt's unit, which while lacking flair was well led.

Bór-Komorowski had no choice but to withdraw into the Old Town. The Home Army held the Bank of Poland, the Town Hall, the Treasury Printing Building and the Royal Castle. Around 170,000 people were crammed into this area of the Old Town, more than twice the normal population. Elsewhere the Home Army held Mokotow and Czerniakow, the city centre and Zoliborz. The Germans set about crushing each of the pockets of resistance.

West of the ghetto, Reinefarth renewed the German attack in the cemetery sector on 8 August. The Poles here numbered about 1,500 men. The Zoska battalion was tasked with defending the Evangelist and Jewish cemeteries. The Broda battalion with three captured tanks was deployed in Okopowa Street, which divided the sector from the ghetto. Other units were in the Calvanist cemetery and Karolkowa Street.

Reinefarth's operation was supported by the guns of an armoured train. A Polish attempt to destroy this was thwarted. German artillery first shelled the vicinity of Okopowa Street, then Reinefarth's infantry backed by tanks and flamethrowers set about the barricades in Zytnia Street. All morning the battle ebbed and flowed.

Once the Germans had captured the Calvinist cemetery, they were able to pin down the Polish units in Okopowa Street. German fire also came from Leszno Street and the ghetto area. Polish losses were heavy and they only just held the Evangelist cemetery. The following day heavy rain dampened down the fighting.

On 11 August the Germans used small remote-controlled tanks, known as Goliaths, for the first time in Okopowa Street. These comprised a tracked demolition charge operated electrically via a cable from another tank. They could carry up to 75 kilos of explosives and were ideal for clearing barricades and other strongpoints. The Germans took the Jewish cemetery but were counterattacked by a Polish battalion when they tried to take the Catholic cemetery. By the end of the day the Germans had cleared two districts and started attacks on the Old Town. The Poles clung to the hope that the Red Army was coming to their aid. However, disturbing reports were filtering in that Polish officers who had reach the Red Army east of the Vistula had been arrested.

The fighting, though, was far from over. There remained a force of about 4,000 Polish fighters in Mokotow, as well as forces of unknown strength in the Old Town and the city centre. Other units were also in the Bielany, Zoliborz and Marymont districts. Another force of about 3,000 had been reported gathering in the forests around Warsaw.

To fend off a wider encircling movement by the Red Army to the north, Field Marshal Model deployed the IV SS Panzer Corps with the 3rd SS and 5th SS divisions moved into blocking positions. From 14 August the Soviets attacked for a week but the SS successfully held off fifteen rifle divisions and two tank corps.

On 19 August the Polish Home Army's efforts to fight reinforcements through to those forces trapped in the Old Town came to nothing. It was clear the defenders would have to be evacuated to the city centre and Zoliborz district. At the end of the month about 2,500 fighters were withdrawn via the sewers, leaving behind their badly wounded. It was then only a matter of time before the SS crushed resistance in the city centre and cleared resistance between the Poniatowski and Kierbedź bridges.

Meanwhile, the Home Army scored a major success on 20 August when it finally overcame the German garrison holding the Warsaw telephone exchange. The Poles killed 38 Germans during the siege of the vast building and took 121 prisoners.

Throughout the city German shelling and mortaring was relentless. The tall Prudential building in the city centre held by the Poles was hit around a thousand times by German artillery. This culminated with an enormous 600mm Karl-Gerät tracked mortar lobbing a 2-ton shell into the building on 28 August. This weapon had started firing ten days earlier. The shells were designed to destroy bunkers and on many occasions after dropping through a building they failed to detonate. The battered and bent Prudential building remained in Home Army hands until the bitter end.

In mid-August Model relinquished his command of Army Group Centre and hastened to France to take charge from Günther von Kluge, in a vain attempt to avert the unfolding German defeat in Normandy. Reinhardt, of 3rd Panzer Army, now found himself leading Army Group Centre, while Generaloberst Erhard Raus took over his old command which withdrew through Lithuania and Kurland.

The great Red Army offensive that commenced in Byelorussia on 23 June 1944 had all but ended by 29 August. By the 26th although the 3rd SS had been forced back to Praga, a counterattack by them on 11 September thwarted another attempt to link up with the Polish Home Army. It was the actions of the 3rd SS and 5th SS that, along with Stalin, consigned Warsaw to two months of bloody agony. The Germans withdrew to the west bank of the Vistula on 13 September and blew up all of Warsaw's bridges.

From 13 September the Red Air Force spent 2 weeks conducting 2,000 supply sorties to the insurgents. The supplies were modest 505 anti-tank rifles, nearly 1,500 submachine guns and 130 tons of food, medicine and explosives. By the time Berling's Polish 1st Army was committed to the battle for Praga time was running out, with Zoliborz under attack by elements of the 25th Panzer Division and just 400 insurgents left holding a narrow strip of the river.

Berling of his own volition recklessly threw his men over the river at Czerniakow but tragically could make no headway. He landed three groups in the Czerniakow and Powiśle areas and made contact with Home Army forces on the night of 14/15 September. He was then forced to withdraw. His men on the eastern shore attempted several more landings over the next four days, but during 15–23 September those who had got over suffered heavy casualties and lost their boats and river crossing equipment.

On 22 September Berling's men were ordered back across the Vistula for a second time. There was hardly any Red Army support and from the 3,000 men who made it across just 900 got back to the eastern shores, two-thirds of whom were seriously wounded. In total Berling's Polish 1st Army losses amounted to 5,660 killed, missing or wounded trying to aid the Warsaw uprising.

After 62 days and having lost 18,000 dead and 25,000 wounded the Polish Home Army surrendered in Warsaw on 2 October. After the surrender 15,000 members of the Home Army were disarmed and sent to prisoner of war camps in Germany. Up to 6,000 fighters managed to slip back into the population with the intention of continuing the fight. The vengeful Himmler, though, expelled the remaining population and ordered the city be flattened.

Crushing the Poles had been a pointless exercise, which cost Hitler 10,000 dead, 9,000 wounded and 7,000 missing. It was clear from the fatalities outnumbering the wounded that no quarter had been given. However, German morale was given a much-needed boost, believing they rather than Stalin had halted Rokossovsky at the very gates of Warsaw.

Poles armed with British-supplied PIAT (Projector, Infantry, Anti-Tank) weapons. These men were posing in the Wola district. The Home Army secured control of half a dozen areas on the western bank of the Volga but failed to consolidate them. The Allies conducted a number of supply flights with mixed results.

A Polish fighter armed with a flamethrower – many of these were home-made by the insurgents. They also created their own hand grenades, mines and submachine guns.

A German Hetzer tank destroyer on the streets of Warsaw. It was captured by the Poles on 3 August 1944.

Hitler and Himmler resolved to crush the Home Army while the Red Army was held at bay to the east of Warsaw. Reinforcements were rushed to the city including SS-Brigadeführer Bronislav Kaminski's anti-partisan brigade. According to SS-Obergruppenführer Erich von dem Bach-Zelewski, they had 'no interest in military discipline'. Kaminski is on the right.

Members of the Dirlewanger Brigade in Focha Street. Bach-Zelewski claimed they 'possessed the highest fighting qualities'.

Officers of Kaminski's Brigade planning their counterattack. This started on 5 August 1944 along Grojecka Street towards Narutowizc Square.

Wacław Micuta Wacek, commander of the Home Army's only tank unit. The Poles used two tanks to liberate Jews still held in the ghetto.

Victims of the Wola massacre. This was perpetrated by Dirlewanger and Kaminski's men. The atrocities in Wola and Ochota culminated in 7,000 people being shot at the Ursus factory. Between 5 and 7 August 40,000 civilians were killed.

Kubuś was the Home Army's only home-made armoured car. Work started on it on 8 August and was finished by 22 August. Built using a Chevrolet van, it was armed with a machine gun and a flamethrower. The vehicle was capable of transporting up to a dozen men and served with the Wydra motorised unit. It was used to support attacks on German positions in Warsaw University on 23 August and again on 2 September. After being damaged during the latter operation it was abandoned four days later.

Above left: German flamethrowers in Leszno Street setting ablaze Warsaw's buildings.

Above right: On 2 October 1944 Bór-Komorowski was forced to surrender. The only concession that he got from the Germans was that all his people would be treated as prisoners of war. It turned out that the women fighters were better off held in Germany than falling into the hands of the rapacious Red Army.

Survivors of the Home Army march off into captivity. In all some 15,000 were taken prisoner.

After the uprising was crushed Hitler demanded what remained of the city be levelled. This included the shell of the Royal Castle which was flattened.

The statue of King Sigismund III in Castle Square toppled by the Germans.

When the Germans withdrew to the west bank of the Vistula on 13 September 1944 they blew up the Kierbedź Bridge. This cut off Warsaw from Praga. They also destroyed the Citadel Rail Bridge to the north and the Poniatowski Bridge.

The beautiful St Alexander's Church and the other buildings surrounding Three Crosses Square were destroyed during the uprising.

Chapter Eight

Soviet Liberation

After enduring two months of terrible bloodletting during the Warsaw uprising, the Poles had to wait another three-and-a-half agonising months before being finally 'liberated' by the Red Army. Hitler had five army groups defending the Eastern Front in January 1945. Army Group Centre held East Prussia and northern Poland along the Narew to the junction with the Vistula. Army Group A was deployed along the middle reaches of the Vistula, from the north of Warsaw down to the Carpathian Mountains.

Warsaw was the responsibility of the German Ninth Army, but holding the city was not a viable option. The garrison comprised just four fortress battalions, one of which was an 'ear battalion' made up of former casualties and invalids, as well as some artillery and engineering units. It was supposed to have been divisional strength but units had been transferred to the Western Front. Nonetheless, Hitler told General Guderian, the German Chief of the General Staff, 'that Warsaw be held at all costs'.

It seemed inevitable that Stalin would strike along the Warsaw–Berlin axis as this was the most direct route to the German capital. Marshal Zhukov's offensive operations were initially dubbed the 'Warsaw–Poznan' operations. Early in 1945 Stalin's Red Army conducted a two-pronged drive on Berlin. Zhukov was to thrust through Poznan in Poland and Konev through Breslau on the River Oder in Germany. Once German forces in East Prussia had been overwhelmed, the Red Army could then advance on Poznan. It was to bypass the city and race toward the Oder, where Hitler was only belatedly trying to create a coherent defensive line. Once over the river Stalin would be at the very gates of Berlin, the Seelow Heights.

Zhukov launched his offensive on 14 January 1945, a day after Konev conducted one from the Baranov bridgehead. For 25 minutes his guns pulverised German defences before advancing from the Magnuszew and Pulawy bridgeheads. Soviet reporter Vasily Grossman, who was with Zhukov's 1st Byelorussian Front, recalled, 'Crossing of the Pilica. We blew up the ice and crossed over on the river bed, thus saving two to three hours.'

The Red Army's 26th Rifle Corps gained a foothold near Warka and the German defenders soon retreated towards Warsaw. The following day Zhukov's right flank attacked north of the city, while other forces pressed towards Warsaw from the southwest. The Soviets captured the airfield at Sochaczew, a town west of Warsaw, and within 24 hours the Red Air Force was operating from it. This was not far from the scene of the Polish army's defeat during the Battle of the Bzura in 1939.

The Warsaw garrison was cut off from Ninth Army. Signals communications were also lost. Hitler designated Warsaw a 'fortress' and demanded that it be held to the last. He also belatedly decided that his forces should go over to the defensive on the Western Front so that reinforcements could be rushed East. However, faced with being trapped, the German garrison commander evacuated the city on 17 January. Before leaving they attempted to blow up anything of use or value in a final needless spasm of wanton destruction.

Stalin gave the honour of liberating Warsaw to the communist Polish forces fighting as part of the Red Army. The Polish 1st Army with Zhukov was given the job of getting into the city. Its 6th Division crossed the Vistula near Praga while the Polish 2nd Division attacked from the north. The 6th Division was given covering fire by the Soviet 31st Special Armoured Train Artillery Battalion. Support was also provided by the Soviet 47th and 61st armies and the Red Air Force.

By midday German troops had been cleared from the city centre. 'When we arrived, liberated Warsaw was looking majestic and sad, even tragic,' wrote Vasily Grossman. 'City streets were filled with heaps of broken bricks.' He visited the remains of the ghetto and saw 'the wall, one and a half times the height of a man, made of red bricks, two bricks thick, with broken glass cemented along the top of it'. Inside he witnessed the flattened buildings and noted, 'The Beast's anger was terrible.' Amid the devastation just two Roman Catholic churches had been left standing.

Guderian in Berlin observed, 'In the late afternoon officers of the Operations Department informed me of the constantly deteriorating situation on the Warsaw front and proposed the establishment of a new defensive line on the premise that Warsaw was already in enemy hands.' He then went to brief Hitler at the Chancellery. During their meeting a message arrived from the Warsaw commandant. According to Guderian, it 'stated that the city was still in German hands but would have to be evacuated in the course of the coming night'.

'They could not possibly have held the city,' said Guderian, 'and would certainly have been taken prisoner if the commandant had obeyed Hitler's orders.' Hitler was furious. Guderian, however, noted that Warsaw was 'only of comparatively minor importance'. For the rest of the conference Hitler remained obsessed with Warsaw and largely ignored all other developments on the Eastern Front. In a fit of petulance, he then sacked the commanders of Army Group A and the Ninth Army and had three colonels from the general staff arrested. To the north two Soviet armies overran 50 per cent of East Prussia and reached the Gulf of Danzig.

Russian and Polish soldiers arriving in Warsaw were shocked to find that from a pre-war population of 1.3 million just 162,000 people remained. There was devastation everywhere. The Germans had flatted the National Library, the Opera House, the Royal Palace and St John's Cathedral. In the Old Town just 6 of its 260 once-magnificent townhouses remained. Through the course of the war it was estimated that three-quarters of the city's buildings had been destroyed. Warsaw had been laid waste. 'Listening to the people from Warsaw tell about Nazi atrocities during the occupation and especially before the retreat,' wrote Zhukov, 'one found it hard to understand the psychology and moral character of the enemy.'

A report was sent to Stalin that stated:

The fascist barbarians have destroyed Warsaw, capital of Poland. With sadistic cruelty the Hitlerites demolished one block of houses after another. The largest industrial enterprises have been razed to the ground. Houses have been either blown up or burnt down. The municipal economy is disrupted. Thousands upon thousands of civilians have been exterminated, the rest driven out. It is a dead city.

Shortly after the liberation Stalin sent Nikita Khrushchev and a team of civil engineers to Warsaw. Their task was to try and restore the power and water supply as well as repair the sewage system. On arrival Khrushchev met the communist Polish government in Praga under Prime Minister Osobka-Morawski and the Mayor General Spychalski. Khrushchev also saw Wladyslaw Gomulka, who became Secretary General of the Polish Communist Party. His team discovered that the power station was still capable of generating electricity and it was possible to pump water. In a short space of time Warsaw got its electricity and water supply back. It was a small step towards recovery.

'Polish officers and men took the destruction of the city especially hard,' said Zhukov. 'I saw battle-scarred Polish soldiers shed tears, and pledge then and there to take revenge on the fiendish foe.' The Polish cities of Cracow and Lodz were liberated on 18 January and two days later Zhukov was over the Silesian border. By 25 January the Red Army had reached Breslau. In Lodz Grossman discovered, 'Five hundred factories and plants. Directors and owners have fled.' Three of them were munitions factories, of which two had been bombed by the RAF. The third had been building torpedoes for the Germans since 1944.

Hitler, losing interest in Poland, decided to move his SS 6th Panzer Army from the Ardennes to Hungary in a ridiculous effort to hold the Hungarian oilfields. He seemed oblivious to the impending destruction of Army Groups A and Centre as well as the growing threat to the Oder. Guderian was flabbergasted, 'The efforts made in Hungary would have proved considerably more effective if carried out on Polish territory or in East Prussia . . .'. Nothing could now stop the Red Army. In early May 1945 after the Battle for Berlin and Hitler's suicide Germany finally surrendered.

Warsaw and the rest of Poland were left to languish under communist rule. The reconstruction of the Polish capital, though, became a national priority. Firstly, there had to be an absolutely enormous clear-up operation. Up to 250,000 men, women and children had died there, along with 18,000 insurgents. There were some 25,000 graves in the streets and squares as well as thousands of bodies in the sewage tunnels. There were also almost 200,000 corpses under the rubble. All had to be removed and given proper burials. The Poles were determined that Warsaw would rise from the ashes and it did eventually in spectacular fashion.

German officers watching the approaching Red Army from the temporary safety of their trench. By early 1945 Hitler was no longer in a position to hold Warsaw. The garrison consisted of just four battalions with limited artillery and engineering support. Their commander, defying orders, decided to evacuate the city.

Triumphant members of the Red Army examining a knocked-out Panther tank. The Red Army and the Polish 1st Army finally liberated Warsaw on 17 January 1945. Hitler was furious it had been lost.

This is what greeted the liberators, an almost derelict city. The Old Town market place was reduced to rubble-strewn ruins.

Above: An aerial view of the wrecked Old Town of Warsaw – to many Soviets it must have reminded them of Stalingrad.

Opposite: By 1944 Warsaw was a ghost town. From a pre-war population of 1.3 million only 162,000 remained. The Germans had almost succeeded in wiping the city from the face of the earth.

Above: Three-quarters of the city's buildings were flattened during the Second World War.

Opposite: Warsaw's damaged buildings left many streets impassable for vehicles.

JÜRGEN STROOP

After the war all those responsible for the destruction of Warsaw were punished. Jürgen Stroop was arrested by the Americans and extradited to Poland. He was hanged in 1952 for his role in crushing the ghetto rising. Bronislav Kaminski was shot by the SS for looting. Oskar Dirlewanger was arrested by the French near Altshausen and died under mysterious circumstances in prison. Reiner Stahel was arrested by the Red Army in Bucharest and spent the rest of his life in prison. Erich von dem Bach-Zelewski testified at the Nuremberg Trials and was not charged with war crimes. He was, though, subsequently sentenced to prison for the murder of political opponents in the 1930s.

Civilians massacred during the ghetto rising. Stroop's meticulous record of his atrocities sealed his fate.

An aging Stroop on trial in Poland in 1951. He showed no remorse for his monstrous actions.

Beds and mattresses thrown on the streets – this illustrates the personal tragedies suffered by the city's inhabitants. The fighting for the city affected everyone.

Above: Warsaw's imposing Krasiński Palace just before the Second World War. Built in 1677–83, it was bordered by manicured gardens and an open square.

Opposite above: The splendour of Krasiński Square. Before the Nazi invasion, Warsaw, a city of culture and learning, was known as the 'Paris of the North'. The Germans put an end to that.

Opposite below: Krasiński Square and the damaged palace, 1945. The German armed forces burned it down.

The destruction and looting of Warsaw was systematic. The Poles, though, vowed to raise their capital city from the ashes and were true to their word.

Further Reading

Borowiec, Andrew, *Warsaw Boy: A Memoir of a Wartime Childhood*, London: Penguin, 2015

Bruce, George, *The Warsaw Uprising*, London: Pan, 1974

Deighton, Len, *Blitzkrieg: From the Rise of Hitler to the Fall of Dunkirk*, London: Jonathan Cape, 1979

Davis, Norman, *Rising '44: The Battle for Warsaw*, London: Macmillan, 2003

Messenger, Charles, *The Art of Blitzkrieg*, Shepperton: Ian Allan, 1991

Orpen, Neil, *Airlift to Warsaw: The Rising of 1944*, Slough: Foulsham, 1984

Shirer, William L., *The Rise and Fall of the Third Reich*, London: Secker & Warburg, 1960

Wernick, Robert, *Blitzkrieg*, New York: Time Life, 1976

The Warsaw Rising Museum, https://www.1944.pl/